WILDFLOWER
GARDENS

60 Spectacular
Plants and How
To Grow Them in
WITHDRAWN Your Garden

C. Colston Burrell-Guest Editor

Coreopsis and culver's root
lupine and miniature lupine

Wildflower Gardens:
60 Spectacular Plants and How to Grow Them in Your Garden

Janet Marinelli
SERIES EDITOR

Jane Ludlam
MANAGING EDITOR

Bekka Lindstrom
ART DIRECTOR

Handbook #159

Copyright © 1999, 2007 (revised edition) by Brooklyn Botanic Garden, Inc.

Handbooks in the *21st-Century Gardening Series* (now *All-Region Guides*)
are published at 1000 Washington Ave., Brooklyn, NY 11225.

Subscription included in Brooklyn Botanic Garden subscriber membership dues
($35 per year; $45 outside the United States).

ISBN 13: 978-1-889538-31-0   ISBN 10: 1-889538-31-0

Printed by OGP in China. Printed on recycled paper.

TABLE OF CONTENTS

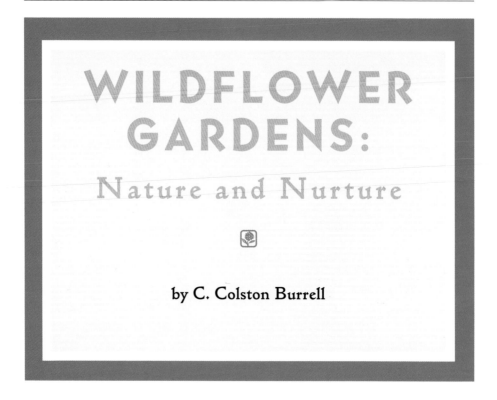

WILDFLOWER GARDENS:
Nature and Nurture

by C. Colston Burrell

ATIVE WILDFLOWERS ARE AMONG the loveliest parts of the natural landscape. They grace fields, woodlands, wetlands, beaches, and rocky mountain slopes. Sweeps of bluebells and trout lilies carpet the ground on a woodland floor. Joe-pye weed and swamp sunflower enliven a moist roadside. In the spring, even the deserts of the Southwest come alive with wildflowers, while in the fall, eastern meadows are awash with goldenrods and asters.

Many wildflowers are also well suited to the cultivated landscape, and there are lots of good reasons to use wildflowers in gardens. Gardeners love color, and we love to bring the beauty of nature into our yards. Growing wildflowers enables us to do both. Another important reason to use native plants is to preserve the character of our regions. The best way to keep the visual sense of place that makes Minneapolis different from Atlanta or Washington, D.C., is to use the local flora. As Wilhelm Miller wrote in his 1915 treatise *The Prairie Spirit in Landscape Gardening*, "The Illinois rose beside the door is beautiful in itself and every year it will come to mean more to every passerby because it will suggest pleasant thoughts of Illinois." The same could be said about other plants and other regions of the country. What's more, native wildflowers

The beauty of many wildflower-strewn natural landscapes, like this lupine field on the rocky slopes near Mount Rainier, is easy to bring home to the garden.

foster and support the maximum diversity of associated plants and animals.

To use wildflowers effectively in the garden, it's not necessary to re-create down to the smallest detail habitats found in nature. This book shows how to incorporate wildflowers in meadows as well as beds and borders and other traditional garden designs. Whether its style is naturalistic or quite formal, however, a wildflower garden should grow out of the site's ecology. "A Gardener's Ecology" covers the ecological processes that should inform the wildflower garden—or any garden. Nature's patterns are also a rich source of inspiration for garden design, and "Designing With Nature" explains how to capture the visual essence of a natural scene by understanding the spatial patterns, both vertical and horizontal, that exist in natural plant communities.

The gardens profiled in the "Portfolio" section are living proof that wildflower gardens can have many styles, from formal to wild. Finally, "The Best American Plants for Wildflower Gardens" profiles the stars of these beautiful landscapes—60 spectacular plants that are adapted to the widest range of garden conditions. For easy reference, the plants are grouped according to their light requirements: shade, partial shade, and sun.

The wildflower garden is evidence of a new garden aesthetic based on regional landscapes and plants, a blend of nature and nurture, and a partnership between a gardener and the forces of nature. Each home landscape is part of the system, and each gardener has a part to play. Ecology can be beautiful.

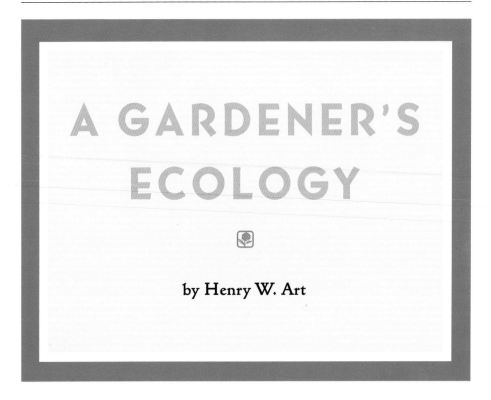

A GARDENER'S ECOLOGY

by Henry W. Art

T HE GROWING INTEREST in wildflower gardens is part of the age-old quest for the "right plant for the right spot." Native plant gardens that are designed to take advantage of local conditions and reflect prevailing ecological processes often are less work than high-maintenance formal beds and borders, and they blend more gracefully into the landscape.

The key to successful wildflower gardening is to keep in mind a few basic ecological considerations, such as variations in local climatic conditions, the structures of plant communities, and soil characteristics. Change is also a natural process that influences wildflower gardens. You should expect that over the long haul weeds will invade, plants will grow, plants will die, and desirable native "volunteers" will find your garden a welcome habitat.

Let Nature Be Your Guide

Naturally occurring plant communities provide the clues to the kinds of wild-flower gardens that might be successful where you live. The natural vegetation varies enormously from region to region, reflecting differences in the

Virginia bluebells are adapted to the sunlight that strikes the floor of this deciduous forest in spring before the canopy leafs out. Look to nearby forests or fields for clues to successful local wildflower gardening.

climate and soils. While a meadow garden of annual wildflowers and grasses may successfully endure for many decades in southern California, it is unlikely to persist for much more than a single growing season in the East. Likewise, it would be nearly impossible to grow a garden of eastern woodland spring perennials in the deserts of the Southwest. Different species are adapted to different sets of environmental conditions, so choose the plants that are going to be most at home in your garden.

Regional patterns of temperature and precipitation play a major role in determining the kinds of vegetation that grow. Forests are generally found in regions with abundant precipitation distributed relatively evenly throughout the year. In forested regions where winter temperatures are cold and the growing season is relatively short, coniferous evergreen forests usually dominate. Deciduous forests with trees that lose their leaves in winter are usually found in regions with milder winters and longer growing seasons. It is obvious to anyone who has seen these two types of forest that the light conditions are dramatically different, as are the wildflowers. While the deciduous forest may cast dense shade during the summer, plenty of light strikes the

The floor of a coniferous forest (left) is shady year-round and wildflowers only grow in sunlit gaps. Prairies receive less rainfall than woodlands and contain a diversity of grasses, wildflowers like Maximilian sunflower, and some shrubs (right).

forest floor in late winter and early spring, and wildflowers proliferate. Coniferous forest, however, casts perpetual shade, and wildflowers tend to grow only in the sunlit gaps where trees have fallen.

Grasslands are found in regions that receive less precipitation than forested areas, and often there are distinct wet and dry seasons, as well as periodic droughts. In North America the transition between forests and prairies begins in the Mississippi River Valley, where annual precipitation is less than about 35 inches. With decreasing amounts of rain and snow, prairie grasses tend to decrease in height, although their roots may penetrate very deeply in search of water. Fire and grazing by large mammals also have played important roles in the maintenance of prairies. Prairies are not just uniform grasses from horizon to horizon; they are extremely diverse plant communities, usually with dozens of different species of perennial (and even some annual) grasses, a great variety of wildflowers, and some shrubs.

Deserts usually receive less than 15 inches of precipitation per year. Like grasslands, they typically have dry and wet seasons, although the wet season may not come every year. In North America the major desert regions extend

A sunny wetland at the edge of a forest (left) is dominated by handsome plants like cottongrass and cinnamon fern. Even the desert is ablaze in spring with wildflowers, like this field of California poppies near Picacho Peak in Arizona (right).

from the Great Basin, between the Sierra Nevada/Cascade Mountains and the Rockies, south into Mexico. The Great Basin deserts have cold winters and are dominated by shrubs like sagebrush, and the warm deserts to the south have mild winters and a greater diversity of shrubs and cacti and other succulents. Periodically, especially during El Niño years, abundant winter precipitation in the desert triggers an amazing display of annual wildflowers in the early spring.

Natural gardeners should take their cue from not only regional vegetation types but also local conditions like topography, drainage, and soil composition. For example, because air temperature decreases as elevation increases, coniferous forests often grow on the higher slopes of mountains in regions that have deciduous forests at lower elevations. Furthermore, at any particular elevation, slopes that face south are sunnier, warmer, and drier than slopes that face north. Slopes that face west are heated by the afternoon sun and therefore tend to be warmer and drier than east-facing slopes. These small differences in topography often lead to large differences in the kinds of vegetation present locally.

Red maple and sugar maple leaves increase soil pH. Choose wildflowers according to your soil conditions.

Topography also influences the drainage conditions at potential garden sites. There tends to be better drainage and drier soils on hill and and ridge tops than at the bottom of slopes. Flat areas at the base of a long slope or near a river may have sufficient water year-round to support distinctive wetland vegetation. Marshes, dominated by grasses and sedges, and swamps, with shrubs and trees adapted to grow in wet soils, are vital environments that regulate floodwater, control pollution, and provide wildlife habitat. While wetland conditions may create challenges for the natural gardener, they also provide opportunities to use the rich palette of species adapted to these habitats.

Sizing Up Soil

An understanding of your soil is essential for successful wildflower gardening. Soil is not just dirt but rather a living medium that consists of particles of different sizes, often varying in mineral composition, air spaces, organic matter, moisture, and creatures ranging from bacteria to earthworms. Sandy soils tend to be dry, since they comprise large grains with relatively big spaces in between—conditions that do not retain moisture very well. Soils rich in clay usually drain poorly, as water cannot pass between the tightly packed, microscopic particles. Different wildflowers are adapted to different soil types. The addition of organic matter improves both soil aeration and its ability to retain moisture.

One of the most important soil factors affecting the growth of wildflowers is pH, a measure of relative acidity or alkalinity. On the pH scale, which ranges from 0 (most acidic) to 14 (most alkaline), 7 is neutral. The pH of a soil results from the chemical composition of the soil minerals but is also influenced by the decomposition of organic matter, the biological activity of soil organisms, and the chemistry of rain or snow falling on the site. In general, soils that form on top of limestone bedrock are more alkaline and have a higher pH than those formed from granite bedrock.

Many wildflowers survive only within a limited pH range, so you should choose species suited to your soil conditions. Keep in mind that the addition of organic matter such as mulch or compost to wildflower gardens can either raise or lower the pH of the soil, depending on the kind of material added. Pine needles, oak leaves, and peat moss tend to acidify the soil, and the leaves of maples and birches make the soil more alkaline.

The Constancy of Change

Plant communities, whether a designed wildflower garden or "natural" vegetation, are constantly changing. Some changes occur on a seasonal or daily basis with various species emerging, flowering, producing fruits, and going into dormancy at different times of the year. In practical gardening terms, this means it is possible to design a wildflower garden with a long season of interest.

Other changes occur over a longer timeline as plant communities respond to disturbances. When a forest is cleared and the land abandoned, it usually does not return immediately to its predisturbance state, but undergoes a gradual recovery through the process of "succession." Fast-growing species with highly mobile seeds are usually the first to arrive. Since many of these species, some of which we call weeds and pull from our gardens, are short-lived and require lots of sun, they are eventually replaced by less mobile, slower-growing species that are adapted to shade. In other words, in forest regions, open land is first colonized by annual grasses and low-growing plants, then perennial wildflowers and shrubs, and eventually various trees. There may be further changes in the species of trees that dominate the recovering forest, with a shift from the aspens and pines that arrive fairly early to oaks, maples, beech, hemlock, or other species that arrive later, are better adapted to growing in the shade, and live longer. Grasslands and deserts have similar stories to tell, but theirs involve different species in the return to predisturbance conditions.

One of the lessons to be learned from succession is that change is a natural ecological process. A meadow garden in a forested region must be periodically disturbed by fire, weeding, or mowing or it will become a forest. However, a meadow in a grassland region may be more easily maintained, since it resembles the natural vegetation.

When designing your wildflower garden, let nature be your guide. The more observant you are of local environmental conditions, the more successful you will be.

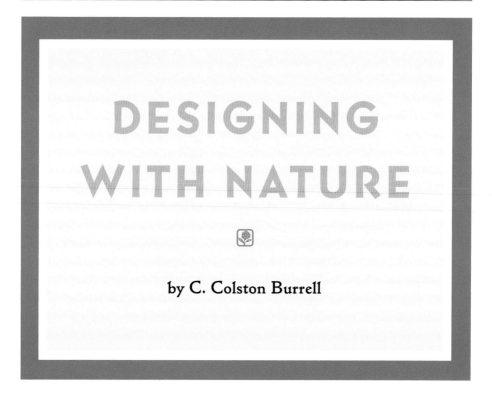

DESIGNING WITH NATURE

by C. Colston Burrell

PATTERNS ARE COMMON in nature. From the shadows cast by dancing leaves to ripples in a pond to overlapping mountain ridges that fade into the haze, natural patterns surround us. In addition to these obvious patterns, there are subtle ones created by the structure of plant communities and the positions plants take in the landscape. Once you understand the factors that create these natural patterns, you can use them to design your wildflower garden.

Vertical Patterns

Every native plant community, whether forest or grassland, wetland or desert, has a discernible structure based on the dominant and subordinant vegetation. The species in any plant community form vertical layers or strata. A forest has a towering canopy of trees that influences what can and cannot grow beneath it. In a maple-basswood forest, for example, the 30- to 100-foot canopy is high and dense, producing a cathedral-like effect. The canopy is interwoven and connected to form a ceiling over the entire forest. The foliage captures much of the light, protects the forest interior

Forests have many layers, including trees that form a ceiling beneath taller canopy trees.

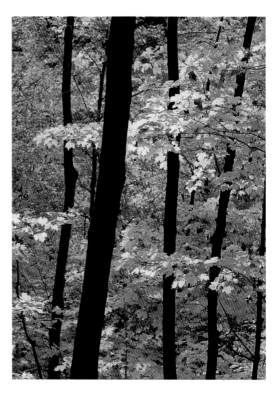

from rapid temperature fluctuations, and cools the air through evapotranspiration.

Smaller trees such as dogwoods and shadblows make up the airy understory. Understory trees from 12 to 30 feet tall form a more intimate ceiling. Beneath these trees is the shrub layer, between 3 and 12 feet above the ground, in scattered patches where light and space are sufficient. The shrub layer is a critical foraging and nesting area for a variety of forest birds. Below the shrubs is the ground layer of wildflowers, grasses, sedges, and ferns. Here, spring ephemerals such as spring-beauty bloom first, followed by taller ferns and persistent species like merrybells.

The age of a plant community affects its distribution, composition, and structure. A young forest often has a well-defined shrub layer and understory. Older forests with dense, closed canopies may have fewer ephemeral plants and more persistent or evergreen wildflowers and ferns. The structure of a forest also varies according to the tree species present. Deciduous forests have the most traditional structure, as described above. By comparison, in a dense woodland of coniferous trees, the understory is very thin, but there is often a thick shrub layer, with herbs and mosses carpeting the ground. Shrub communities have mixed layers of different-sized shrubs, with a ground layer of herbs, grasses, and sedges.

In meadows, prairies, and other communities dominated by herbaceous plants, the vertical structure is no less distinct. However, unlike the trees and shrubs in forests, the plants must resprout from their roots each year. The earliest plants to emerge in the spring, such as violets, are short. Each

The patterns of a prairie landscape, dominated by grasses and herbs, can be re-created in a garden. A miniature meadow blankets a sunny backyard with dazzling wildflowers like purple coneflower and black-eyed susan.

successive wave of plants to emerge overtops the next, culminating with the tallest grasses and late-blooming composites, such as sunflowers and asters.

Horizontal Patterns

Plants within a given community are also distributed in horizontal patterns on the landscape as a result of environmental factors such as soil, moisture, and light. Different species thrive with various amounts of moisture. In a prairie, shrubs grow in the wettest areas, whereas grasses and herbs grow in the slightly higher and drier areas. On ridges, species of smaller stature that cannot compete with the taller lowland vegetation dominate.

In deciduous forests, the dry, sunny ridges support oaks and hickories, while maples and basswood grow in the moister coves in loamy soil on eastern and northern slopes. Individual trees are spaced according to their canopy size and shape. Between the trees, shrubs may abound or be absent. The distribution of species in the ground layer is dependent on subtle changes in light, slope, elevation, exposure, and soil moisture. In wetlands,

Tree trunks naturally dominate the design of a woodland garden. Native wildflowers, such as Rocky Mountain columbine, can be used to brighten the ground layer in a garden where deciduous trees cast shade during part of the year.

sedges dominate the wettest areas, shrubs the intermediate regions, and prairie or woodland plants the drier uplands. Each species occupies its own niche within the community.

The Big Picture

To reap maximum ecological benefits, think of your garden as part of a landscape matrix that connects your yard with your neighbors', one neighborhood with another, and your town with the surrounding countryside. Visualize this matrix as an interconnected web and you can see how each home's landscape has a profound influence on the rest of the natural community.

Within your yard you can create a garden in harmony with its surroundings to keep the matrix intact. Locate lawns close to the house, and plant an area of turf no larger than the space you need for family barbecues or summer games of croquet. This is the part of your yard that will be lowest in diversity of plants and associated wildlife. Create a shallow depression where water can infiltrate instead of running off of lawns and paths and eventually into nearby waterways, where it can cause erosion and pollution. Also place ornamental and vegetable gardens near the house, perhaps bordering the lawn; consider confining nonnative plants to this portion of the garden. If your lot is large, with more space than you need for gardening and recreation, consider a small-scale restoration of the native habitat. You may choose a meadow, prairie, or woodland, based on existing conditions and your region of the country. When linked with wildflower gardens in neighboring yards, these can help reconnect the matrix so that plants and animals aren't trapped in isolated islands in a vast urban or suburban sea.

Next consider the planting design. To start, it helps to visualize a favorite place in the woods or fields and sketch the scene, trying to capture something of the visual quality of the place. If the special place is a woodland, tree trunks will no doubt dominate the picture. In a prairie or meadow, the sea of grasses or scattered clumps of shrubs will create the scene. This exercise will reveal the major structural components and types of plants that give a place its unique character. Understanding this character is fundamental to designing with nature.

To re-create a natural scene in your garden, you must first duplicate or approximate the visual-essence species—those plants that are present in the greatest numbers or that dominate the vertical structure of the plant community. In a woodland it is the tall, dark trunks of trees, those species without which you would not have the woods. To maximize the ecological complexity of your wildflower garden, you must imitate this vertical structure. Layering adds visual as well as ecological complexity. The canopy creates a monumental feeling. The understory brings the enclosure down to an intimate level, like the ceiling of a living room. Shrubs divide spaces, screen views, and create enclosures. The ground layer, like the furnishings of a room, offers the variety and seasonal interest that all keen gardeners crave.

In a garden modeled on a grassland, tall grasses can take the place of shrubs. These grasses and tall, herbaceous wildflowers are like translucent screens, whereas dense wildflowers, such as cup plants and joe-pye weed, form solid walls in summer that become see-through in winter.

The wildflower garden does not have to be a reconstruction of nature, however. The design may be highly ordered. A pergola can substitute for tree trunks, with vines forming the canopy. Hedges can be the shrub layer. The point is to represent nature in a form that reflects your individual aesthetic but still functions ecologically.

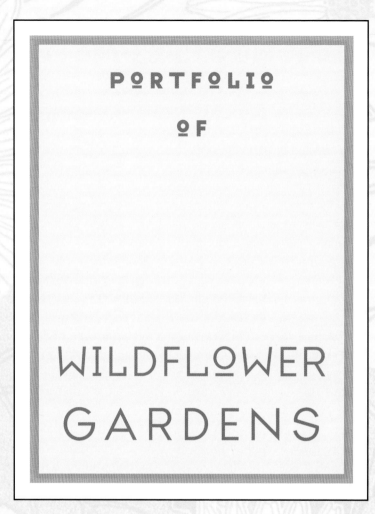

PORTFOLIO

OF

WILDFLOWER

GARDENS

BEDS AND BORDERS

by Kim Hawks

Beds and borders liberated me as a gardener, transforming my yard into a garden filled with a diversity of plants. Within my beds grow trees, shrubs, herbs, and perennials—including many native North American wildflowers. I plant annuals only sparingly.

Among my goals for the garden was an informal style—almost a wild look. I have learned from observing nature's gardens that plants grow in layers and have adopted this look in my garden. Spring ephemerals are followed by summer herbaceous plants, overlaid with a loose canopy of shrubs and small trees. I've also learned that in the wild, plants like to be in the company of other plants. Rather than leave neat, barren spaces between perennials, I use the recommended spacing for each plant and intersperse annual or biennial natives in bare areas.

Encouraging wildlife in the garden, especially butterflies, birds, and dragonflies, was also important to me, along with reducing my acre or so of turf to a much smaller area. All of these goals were achieved when I began creating borders and free-form island beds.

One way to unify such a garden is to design walkways and beds simultaneously; a path emerges and each bed begins to relate to the others. Another way I tie together my garden is by randomly repeating certain plants throughout all the beds. These "signature" plants draw the eye from one bed to the next and create a unifying whole. Examples in my garden include purple verbena, switchgrass, and artemisia.

ADDING WILDFLOWERS

I enjoy bringing wild plants into the garden. Although the bottom line for me is not a plant's origins but whether it has what I'm looking for (purple flowers, say, or nectar for butterflies), my selection often turns out to be a North American native.

The differences between using native or more traditional, exotic perennials are minimal but merit discussion. Some gardening books advise us to feed perennials regularly, or at least to amend the soil at planting time with organic matter, including copious amounts of

Wildflower beds and borders, unified by paths and the repetition of plants throughout the garden, support a diversity of plant and animal life.

manure. However, if you prepare an overly rich soil, many sun-loving native perennials become lush monsters and outgrow themselves. Some gardeners believe that native perennials do not require any soil preparation or other coddling. The truth lies somewhere between overindulgence and neglect. Always start by selecting a plant that will thrive in your existing soil. If you are planting a native perennial that was propagated in a nursery, most likely it has been grown in a soilless medium. It hasn't experienced the soils of local fields or roadsides, so

it needs assistance getting established. Plant your new native in a loosened soil amended with organic matter and mulch, and water it regularly until it becomes established.

I've also discovered that many wildflowers indigenous to wet areas tolerate slightly drier sites in cultivation. For instance, joe-pye weed inhabits sunny, wet ditches. Yet it thrives in my garden in a sunny, well-drained area that receives supplemental watering in dry times. However, the reverse is not true: Plants that inhabit dry, lean locations do not like soggy soils.

A striking combination: winecups and Texas bluebonnets.

MIXING UP THE PLANTING

Unless its defining characteristic is its smallness, a border made up exclusively of herbaceous perennials can be the highest-maintenance area of the garden. For this reason, in my borders and island beds I incorporate compact or dwarf shrubs, small ornamental trees, and vines. Woody plants also offer multiseasonal color in their foliage, fruits, and flowers. American beautyberry, for example, has striking purple berries that spiral around the stems like amethyst beads. Small to medium native ornamental

trees include snowbell, redbud, and pink-flowering dogwood.

Draw attention to your beds and borders by combining plants with sharply different foliage, texture, or form. Keep the composition slightly off balance by using some plants in large numbers and others in arrangements of one or three. For example, switchgrass has a loose, vertical structure four or five feet tall, and in the fall its showy seed heads add an airy quality. Combine this native grass with the bold, six- to seven-foot-tall joe-pye weed with its rounded mauve flowers, and you've got a striking contrast. To reinforce the vertical lines, add some cabbage-leaf coneflower, with its rockets of yellow flowers atop stems reaching four to seven feet. Garden phlox repeats in miniature the rounded form of joe-pye weed; it tops out at four feet and blooms three to four weeks before it, along with four-foot purple coneflower. Southern blue flag iris rounds out this composition with its boldly vertical, four-foot-high foliage and violet-blue, yellow-splotched flowers.

I place fragrant plants near the edge of the beds where they can be enjoyed. I also plant white flowers or variegated plants along the edges to illuminate the paths in the evening. Great wildflowers to light the way include the early-summer-flowering white garden phlox and dwarf fothergilla, which offers numerous white bottlebrush-like flowers early in the season. Mountain mints offer cool, silvery foliage—deliciously fragrant when touched—amid tiered, usually white (depending on the species) flowers.

WILDFLOWERS AND WILDLIFE

One of my favorite island beds has a meadow theme and is home to native wildflowers that grow five to eight feet tall. Here I have learned how to garden with aggressive plants, placing "aggressives with aggressives" and letting them work out their own balance. Wildflowers in this bed include joe-pye weed, cabbage-leaf coneflower, various powdery mildew-resistant bee balms, mountain mints, and goldenrods.

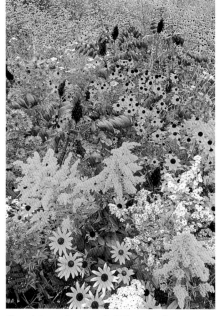
Combine plants of different forms.

My entire garden is planted with wildflowers for butterflies, which naturally flock to these dependable, nectar-rich natives. Plant a wide diversity of native wildflowers to provide nectar throughout the seasons. Native sunflowers, coneflowers, butterfly weed, black-eyed susans, blazing stars, asters, and joe-pye weed are among the wildflowers that offer plentiful nectar.

Resist the temptation to cut back flowering stems the moment the blossoms wilt and you will be rewarded with your own living bird feeders. Birds are particularly attracted to the seeds of asters, black-eyed susans, coreopsis, blazing stars, and goldenrods. When ripe flower heads disperse their seeds, however, you may end up with unwanted seedlings. Scratch them out early and the task will not seem overwhelming.

Layers of native wildflowers enhance garden beds and borders. Your yard will not only be more beautiful, it also will celebrate your particular region—be it the mountains, the desert, the plains, or, as in my case, the Piedmont.

SHADE GARDENS

by Carole Ottesen

As a rule, gardeners don't seek out shade. Eventually and inevitably, shade happens. Slim saplings grow stout, casting ever-larger, leafy patterns over lawn and border. Suddenly one fine day, there it is: The yard is all shade. Tomatoes and zinnias are no longer possibilities. However, this new reality makes it possible to embark on one of gardening's most gratifying adventures: A wildflower garden in the shade. The best model for the design of such a garden is a native woodland.

LAYING THE GROUNDWORK

The connection between forest and shade garden is more than merely visual. Processes that occur in a woodland are also at work in a shaded yard. In a woodland, leaves, plant litter, twigs, and branches decompose slowly into humus that builds up the deep, friable, moisture-retentive soil favored by forest plants.

To re-create this rich-soil environment in a garden, you can gather the leaves, branches, and litter and compost them before top-dressing garden beds—a labor-intensive project that has the advantage of looking neat. The alternative is to practice a modified kind of "sheet composting"—allowing litter to decompose in place, made tidy, if necessary, with a cover of mulch or chopped leaves. Sheet composting is a good way to make a garden bed out of a lawn that no longer receives enough sun to support lush grass. Several inches of leaf litter covering the prospective bed in fall will kill the grass beneath. In warm spells throughout the fall, winter, and early spring, the pile of organic matter will decompose, beginning the transformation of ordinary garden soil into something more like the humus-rich soil of a woodland. Earthworms help the process along, enriching the soil with their castings.

SHADES OF SHADE

Plants in a woodland layer themselves as they compete for light—from the tops of forest trees to understory trees down to shrubs and herbaceous plants. In the shade garden, it makes sense to group plants accordingly, where light is

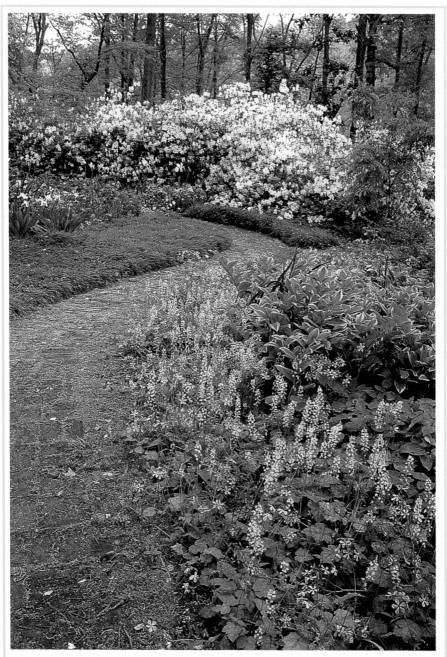

In a shady garden, wildflowers such as woodland phlox, foamflower, and solomon's seal fringe a meandering path.

SHADE GARDENS

Subdued light accents the discreet texture and hues of unfurling bloodroot.

most abundant. When herbaceous wildflowers are placed with understory trees and shrubs on the bright side of large trees and in a fringe along path openings, the result looks spontaneous and natural.

The choice of plants for the shady wildflower garden is limited only by the amount of light or lack of it. Most shade gardens possess a range of light intensity, from partial shade—just a hair too shady to grow sun-loving plants—to deep shade— where no direct sunlight penetrates. In between these extremes is medium, or dappled, shade, where the sun filters teasingly through moving leaves of the tree canopy, and high shade, a place with bright light but no direct sun. Summer, when the tree canopy is at its fullest, is the best time to map out a garden's degrees of shade and select corresponding plants for each area.

Short of removing them entirely, limbing up trees is the classic method of increasing light in a woodland. Gardeners do this to achieve partial shade, which has a wide realm of potential plant inhabitants. Because most plants tolerate a range of light conditions, virtually all shade-loving plants and quite a few sun lovers will grow and thrive in partial shade.

SHADY CHARACTERS

Fortunately, there is no dearth of shade-loving plants to occupy parts of the garden in medium to deep shade. Spring ephemerals such as Virginia bluebell and trilliums thrive in any part of a shady garden, because they receive all the light they need in early spring before the trees leaf out. By late spring when the tree canopy fills out, they die down, completing the active part of their life cycle before going dormant in summer. Along with the wood phloxes, ephemerals provide the earliest color and interest. Later arrivals such as baneberry and bottle gentian can be planted beside ephemerals so that when they die down, their spaces will be filled with plants that carry on until fall.

For new gardens, some of the most versatile and forgiving plants are wood poppy, wild geranium, and wild gingers. They tolerate a range of conditions and establish quickly, eventually spreading into seamless groundcovers that discourage weeds. Massed in groundcover, these plants provide rich texture—a valuable commodity in any garden but especially welcome and fitting in a shady one. Subdued light renders a shady garden serene; in this peaceful atmosphere, subtleties like the patterns and rhythms of texture become dominant features.

Likewise, in the shade, a little color goes a long way. While gentle light accentuates the contrasts and nuances among the greens and variegations of foliage, the bold-colored flowers that thrive in sunny gardens may appear jarringly out of place in the shade. Appropriately, many of the perennials for shade are discreetly hued. In spring, a shady garden glows with the blues of dwarf crested iris, Virginia bluebell, and jacob's ladder, and the whites of the great white trillium, baneberry, and bloodroot.

Adding summer color to the shady garden requires a bit more guile. One small break in the tree canopy, natural or fabricated, will admit shafts of sunlight to support one or two vibrantly hued plants. A hot spot of red in a sea of greens makes up in intensity for what is not possible in number. Cardinal flower, which holds its scarlet blooms aloft in late summer, is an excellent candidate for this role. Red- and fuchsia-colored bee balm work equally well.

Gardening in the shade is different from gardening in full sun. It is cooler and more comfortable, but it is accomplished only in full cooperation with nature and with a watchful eye on the tree canopy. Fortunately, there is an exceedingly choice coterie of plants to choose from. While it can be challenging, it has more than its share of rewards.

WATER AND BOG GARDENS

by Madeleine Keeve

*Water is H₂O, hydrogen two parts,
oxygen one, but there is also a third
thing that makes it water, and
nobody knows what this is.*
— D.H. Lawrence, "The Third
Thing," *Pansies*, 1929

Just as a good gardener reveres soil as an integral part of a garden's complicated existence, so a good pond keeper appreciates a body of water as an active ecosystem that supports all manner of organisms—not just plants. Unlike a swimming pool, a water garden teems with life.

If you have a pond, stream, or boggy area on your property, you have a special opportunity to create a garden habitat that works with nature. You control the design of a water garden, but the control is actually a kind of stewardship, an appreciation of what nature can do better than any gardener. If you are sure to use plants suited to your water environment, the garden will thrive.

AQUATIC AND BOG PLANTS

Aquatic plants, such as water-lilies and pickerel weed, that grow in still water, and bog plants, such as marsh mallow, which grow in water-logged soil, are easy to cultivate once you become familiar with their native habitats and locate them in suitable areas of the garden. Open areas in full sun are the natural habitats for many aquatic and bog plants. However, while few true aquatics do well in shade, quite a few bog plants thrive there.

Light exposure isn't the only consideration when choosing plants for the garden. Different watery conditions also present various opportunities for a range of plants. Aquatics flourish in the placid waters of a pool or pond. The moving water of a stream can't sustain aquatics, but it can support rich plant growth along its banks. The constant presence of moisture on the shady edge of a stream allows you to grow many ferns and wildflowers, including lobelia and foamflower, as well as shrubs such as winterberry, redtwig dogwood, and swamp azalea. A naturally wet area in your garden, such as a spring-fed ditch or a low-lying area with poor drainage, is a perfect spot for some North American native iris or the curious woodlander jack-in-the-pulpit.

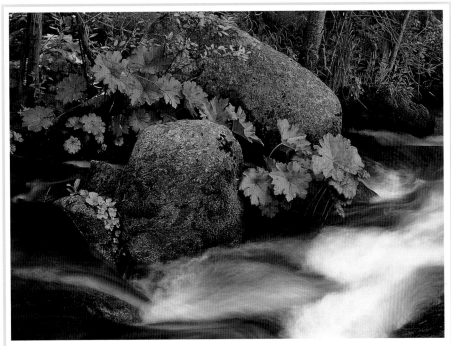

Umbrella leaf flourishes on the banks of a stream of rushing water.

Before choosing plants for a water or bog garden, acquaint yourself with the soil at the site: Is it sandy, heavy clay, or rocky? Do the edges stay dry or waterlogged all season? Does your boggy area go bone dry in August? Such factors will inform your decisions about which plants to pick and where they will go.

Next, learn about the plants you'd like to cultivate: their native range, hardiness, preferred growing conditions, ultimate size, how quickly they grow and multiply, and whether or not they attract birds or insects. Many plants are polite growers, or easily restrained, but some, such as horsetail (*Equisetum fluviatile*) may be aggressive or even invasive in your area, even if they are native to North America. Consult local experts to make sure that any plant you introduce will not escape into nearby natural areas and become a pest.

DESIGN CONSIDERATIONS

The constant presence of water allows aquatic and bog plants to produce lush foliage with well-defined shapes and often a reflective, water-repellent sheen. Choose these plants on the merits of their

The bold color and striking leaves of blue flag iris unify pond and garden.

leaves as well as their flowers, which often come and go quickly. Water-lilies, skunk cabbage, and hardy water canna (*Thalia dealbata*), among other plants, have large, beautifully shaped leaves with a bold, almost tropical presence that provide interest even when the plants are out of flower.

When it comes to plants in a pond or bog, fewer is better. The ecology of a healthy pond or pool requires that roughly one-third to one-quarter of the water's surface remains free of plant cover. While that may seem like an awful lot of open space, remember that a body of still water is a flat, shining surface, reflecting the sky and surrounding vegetation. Be sure to keep this in mind when designing your water garden. Any reflective surface, whether water or mirror, makes everything look larger, and so each plant in a pond or pool will appear double in size.

Even in a small space, however, locate at least one large plant with a strong presence, such as the native umbrella leaf (*Diphylleia cymosa*), in or near the water. One or two large plants allied with a few smaller companions creates a more pleasing effect than a variety of small plants—they will only look chaotic, and make no impression when viewed from a distance.

When choosing plants for a water and/or bog garden, don't think of them as individual specimens but rather as communities: Shade-tolerant plants belong in one area and sun lovers in another. Then, within each community, group plants with an eye toward interesting combinations of size, leaf shape, color, and texture. For example, the majestic leaves of western skunk cabbage might dominate a boggy area; smaller plants with markedly different leaves such as marsh marigold and bellwort would be good companions—all are tolerant of partial shade and flower in early spring. Each plant in the threesome contributes leaves and flowers of different sizes and shapes, but the flowers of all three are shades of yellow, unifying the composition.

While the plants are still in containers, experiment with their placement. You might even set the pots in a test arrangement, leave them for a while, then return at another time of day or view them from another direction to see if the combination still pleases you.

As in any naturalistic garden, the great constant in the water gar-

Marsh marigold's bright color lights up wet sites in partial shade.

den is change: The amount of light changes with the seasons, temperatures rise and fall, and plants emerge, flower, and die back. Learn to work with these changes to foster an environment you will treasure in all seasons. You'll enjoy not only the plants you've arranged but also the dynamics of a thriving ecosystem—fish leaping up to catch mosquitoes; dragonflies and birds flitting among the greenery, frogs croaking love songs at dusk. If D.H. Lawrence had been a water gardener, he'd have recognized, in the hullabaloo, that third thing.

WATER AND BOG
GARDENS

MEADOW AND PRAIRIE GARDENS

by Joan Feely

It's a late June day, and the coneflowers, culver's root, and spiderworts are in their glory. The seed heads of cool-season grasses are backlit by the setting sun as they sway in the warm breeze. As you walk along your meadow path, butterflies abandon their flowers to seek out the salty perspiration on your brow, American goldfinches scatter at your approach, and the kids race ahead to find the box turtle that they glimpsed the day before.

With their promise of just this sort of scene, meadows and prairies have inspired a new and appealing garden style. Gardens modeled on meadows and their closely related Midwestern counterparts, prairies, are less polluting than the high-care lawns they often replace yet retain the openness of manicured turf. The diverse plant life of these wildflower-filled grasslands supports a wide array of animals close at hand, flying about at eye level and scurrying around the next sunflower.

Lady Bird Johnson's efforts to reintroduce bluebonnet and Indian paintbrush to the Texas roadsides have inspired gardeners across America. Unfortunately, the annuals that make the Texas roadsides so beautiful are native to that state and don't grow well in other parts of the United States. In order to recreate the colorful displays along the Texas roadsides in places such as North Carolina, Maryland, and Ohio, landscape designers often rely on annuals and biennials from California and Europe. This has led to the birth of the "instant meadow." These artificial meadows have little value to native wildlife, must be replaced each year, and require more work than perennial beds. In the Midwest and East at least, the showy wildflowers are perennials, not annuals and biennials as they are in the arid West.

You need to look locally for the natural model and the appropriate plants for your grassland garden. Every region in the United States has splendid, natural meadowlike habitats dominated by grasses and adorned with wildflowers of every description, from delicate lilies to monstrously tough and tall rosinweed (growing to 12 feet in moist prairies!). Any garden can include a

In its second year, a beautiful meadow planting of native wildflowers in Iowa has come into its own and needs little maintenance or extra water.

MEADOW AND PRAIRIE GARDENS

meadow component, whether it be a sidewalk strip for a city garden or a multi-acre swath on a sprawling property.

MEADOW DESIGN

Designing a meadow is much like designing any garden. The first order of business is deciding where it is going to go. The site must have at least eight hours of direct sun. Soils that are not overly fertile produce the best results, as they support fewer weeds.

When selecting species to include in your meadow, start with dessert—the wildflowers. Think in terms of choosing plants suited to your topography and soil, as well as the individual wildflower's season of bloom; after the meadow is established, watering, pruning, and deadheading should be unnecessary. Buy your plants and seeds from nurseries close to home, which are more likely to stock species adapted to your environmental conditions.

It's helpful to create a base map that delineates the topographic variation and the soil moisture levels of your site. Using a set of four or five transparencies that overlay one another will help you visualize the seasons of bloom. Make separate sheets for spring, early summer, high summer, fall, and winter.

Aim for 20 to 30 wildflower species. To achieve a natural look, keep in mind that in most prairies and meadows, the dominant wildflowers are daisy relatives such as asters, coneflowers, sunflowers, and goldenrods. Legumes make up the next largest group, including the indigos, native clovers, partridge pea, and wild lupine. In moisture-retentive soils, bee balm and spiderwort will thrive, along with queen-of-the-prairie and giant meadow rue. Don't forget the milkweeds (*Asclepias* species), which are essential to the monarch butterfly's life cycle.

The grasses in your meadow or prairie garden set it apart from the traditional perennial garden. They can be divided into two simple categories: tall and short. Generally, the taller grasses prefer moderately moist soils; the shorter grasses, drier soils. Place the tallest species—big bluestem, Indian grass, purple top, and eastern gama grass—toward the center or rear of the garden. Smaller grasses such as little bluestem, broom sedge, purple lovegrass, and prairie dropseed accent the showy wildflowers.

There are two basic approaches to arranging meadow plants. Scattering the different species throughout the site will create a fine-textured garden that invites

In areas where homeowners have traditional turf lawns, it helps to keep the peace among neighbors by mowing the edges of a wildflower meadow.

closer inspection, but be sure to sprinkle together species that bloom at the same time for the best show. Another approach is to group species in masses, providing denser splashes of color for your pleasure—and easy targets for nectar-seeking hummingbirds and butterflies.

When designing a meadow garden, it is important to create a sense of intent. A rustic fence along the perimeter, a cleanly mown edge, or a beautiful sculpture announces to the neighbors that someone is caring for the garden, that in this place something enticing is going to happen.

HOW-TOS

You must control the undesirable plants at the site before planting a meadow garden. Planting directly into sods of Kentucky bluegrass or zoysia will not result in a thriving garden, and overseeding turf will result in total failure. Only in a lawn of native grasses should you plant into existing turf.

If a pampered lawn is to be converted to meadow, a year of grow-

MEADOW AND PRAIRIE GARDENS

Purple coneflower and prairie clover are lovely native prairie wildflowers.

number of native biennials such as black-eyed susan can be included in the seed mix to color up the first years. If weeds are a problem, cut the meadow to six inches; this won't harm the young seedlings but will reduce weed seed production. Sowing grass seed in late spring or early summer and adding wildflower plants in the fall will result in a mature meadow in less time.

Once the meadow takes hold, basic maintenance consists of an annual mowing, done in the winter, if possible. If your meadow backs up to a woodland, special attention must be paid to the woodland edge, because birds perched there will plant various fleshy-fruited species, such as Japanese honeysuckle, bittersweet, and mulberry, to name a few. Remove these weedy species as soon as possible, as they have the potential to overrun your grassland.

ing the lawn with no fertilizer while continuing to mow will help use up the excess nutrients that benefit weeds more than desired wildflowers. Methods for clearing the ground include covering smaller areas with black plastic, applying herbicides, and using a sod cutter. The first two methods require a full year of treatment to control both cool- and warm-season plants.

A meadow garden can be started with seed, plants, or a combination of both, depending on your budget and how long you can wait for your meadow garden to bloom. Wildflowers planted from seed will bloom after three years. A small

When you create a meadow, you are creating the most basic sustainable landscape. Nature will have an important role to play, determining in large part the ultimate density of your wildflowers, the lushness of your grasses, the height of your joe-pye weed. As many a gardener has discovered, a meadow or prairie garden is a true partnership with nature.

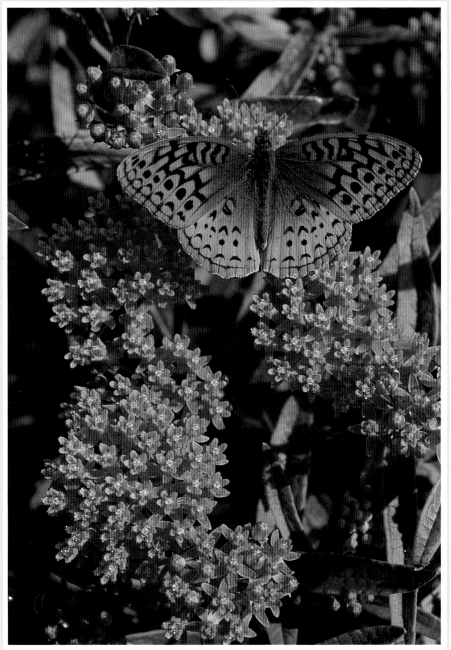

Wildflower species like butterfly weed grown in masses provide splashes of color and are easy targets for butterflies, such as this fritillary.

MEADOW AND
PRAIRIE GARDENS

HELL STRIPS AND ROCKERIES

by James Stevenson

Rushing in to create a garden where angels fear to tread may seem like a foolish endeavor, but to the plant enthusiast, no patch of ground can be left untouched. Such is the case with the hell strip—an area that is inaccessible to regular maintenance, has poor soil, or is exposed to heat, cold, punishing wind, or other extreme conditions.

A hell strip could be the area between the sidewalk and the road, along a fence outside your garden, or between the parking lot and the garage. It could be an island surrounded by pavement, a ditch, or a berm—anywhere attempts to beautify are challenged by the site's unpleasantness. Or perhaps your hell strip is a "rockery"—a pile of concrete or bricks from a past project or a natural stone outcropping.

Most gardeners clothe their hell strips in turf and maintain them with the mower or lawn trimmer, or plant a bank of low-maintenance groundcover. However, if it is highly visible, a bit of inspired design may be called for. And if you really think it through and make careful plant choices, you can have a garden area that requires little maintenance.

LOOK TO NATURE

Rather than trying to "fight the site" with costly manipulation of soil and water conditions, plant your hell strip with species suited to the existing conditions. Base your plant selections on the native plant communities that grow on similar sites. Just because black-eyed susan is native to your area doesn't mean that it will thrive in the shaded muck in your backyard; its native habitat is poor soils in full sun. Look instead to the plant communities in your region that grow naturally in moist, shaded places.

I have even drawn inspiration from gas stations and fast-food restaurants for plants that will withstand extreme conditions. Though seemingly untended, these plants manage to thrive and color the landscape (often matching the lurid palette of the business they adorn). For example, the thread-leaf yucca (*Yucca filamentosa*) always seems thrilled to rise up out of burgundy-colored pumice mulch. Think of

Moss phlox is a low-growing wildflower that makes an excellent lawn alternative and can beautify a rocky site where other plants might languish.

incorporating the survivors you find in your area with tough-as-nails native annuals and perennials for a mixed planting ready to take on the elements. Combining tough woody plants with seasonally showy wildflowers and perennials can create an enviable display with a modicum of maintenance.

Part of the fun is deciding what effect you want to create throughout the year. Perhaps you want a big, audacious bounty of bloom all summer long, doubling as a screen or barrier. Large wildflowers and grasses suit this design well, and the grasses such as panic grass (*Panicum virgatum*) remain upright and create a screen through the winter as well. Or maybe you want a lawn alternative made of short, flowering plants. In this case, moss phlox, poppy mallows, sundrops, and native sedums and wallflowers are a few plants to consider.

Some hell strips call for perennials that can take abuse, such as indigos and lupines with dramatic spires of blue, white, or yellow flowers and a lovely spherical outline of foliage the rest of the year. A choice cultivar, *Baptisia* × 'Purple Smoke', combines

HELL STRIPS AND ROCKERIES

Purple coneflower (left) lures butterflies to sites where many plants fear to tread. White wild indigo (right) also withstands extreme conditions.

the charcoal stems of the white-flowering species with the blue-violet flowers of wild blue indigo.

Among the early-flowering perennials you may wish to inter-plant specimens whose foliage holds appeal year-round. Tough types like the native prairie sage (*Artemisia ludoviciana*) lend foliar interest between floral displays. Many ornamental grasses are also perfectly suited to extreme environ-ments. Large species, such as the upright panic grass, are best rele-gated to the back of a planting.

In summer, a plethora of won-derful wildflowers reigns. Purple coneflowers provide great garden presence as well as a wealth of nec-tar for butterflies. Black-eyed susan can certainly stand its ground in a hell strip, combining well with the creeping North American native *Verbena canadensis*, which creates a hazy purple groundcover all sum-mer long. The cabbage-leaf cone-flower towers in bloom to four to seven feet. The flower's central black cone is set off by the droop-ing golden-yellow petals, but its

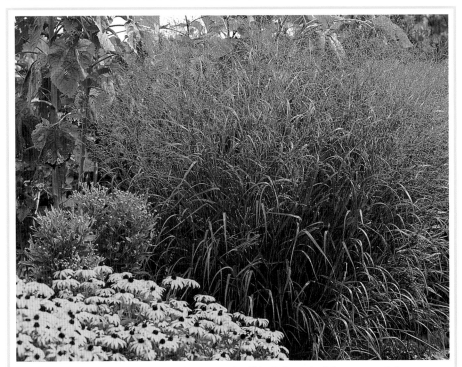

Grasses like panic grass grow dense and tall in inhospitable areas of the garden, providing color and texture and acting as a screen all summer.

wide blue-gray foliage is reason enough to grow it.

Fall belongs to the asters and goldenrods. Asters come in a range of colors, all harmonious in the slanting rays of sunlight at the end of the year. Goldenrods have long been blamed for causing hay fever, but this is not so. What they do cause is "oohs" and "aahs" when the burst of golden flowers arrives on the scene.

ROOTING AROUND A ROCKERY

Like the hell strip, a rockery is a challenging and fun site to gussy up. It may be a ruin of rubble or rocks or a stacked-stone retaining wall, complete with nooks and crannies perfect for tucking in little plant treasures.

Choosing plants for my own sunny rockery was easy. I am a rabid crocophile, and I planted as many of the little species crocuses as I could get my hands on. Instead of planting them in drifts, I planted pockets of five or so bulbs in the spaces between rocks and around the base. Many traditional rock garden plants suffer in our humid

HELL STRIPS AND ROCKERIES

North Carolina summers, so to a great extent I turned once again to the native plant communities to search for those adapted to our climate. Locating a nursery source for one of my favorite spring flowers, bluet (*Houstonia serpyllifolia*), was a happy day. It creates a spreading mat of foliage festooned with little blue stars in spring and summer and does not go dormant but rather persists as a foliage plant when out of bloom. Stargrass (*Hypoxis hirsuta*) blooms in early summer with cheerful yellow stars on slender stems. Though stargrass is found in the woods and in edge situations, it seems perfectly happy out in the sun.

An extraordinary little native American perennial is bluestar (*Amsonia tenuifolia* var. *filifolia*). As its incredibly fine-textured, light green foliage froths out of the rocks, it looks like Easter-basket grass that has blown into the garden. In spring, light blue star-shaped flowers are displayed at the tips of the wiry stems. On the same scale and contrasting with bluestar is another native, green-and-gold (*Chrysogonum virginianum*), which has paddle-shaped, dark green leaves and one- to two-inch golden flowers. As the beauty of its display peaks in April, green-and-gold is not particularly long-lived, but it does grow rapidly.

A wall can be a fun place to situate plants that will reseed themselves in the crevices. I have seen *Corydalis* species appear, clinging to a vertical slope between wall stones. This is due to the fact that their seeds are dispersed by ants, who can navigate this gravitationally tricky terrain. Other ant-dispersed native wildflowers include wild bleeding heart (*Dicentra eximia*) and wake-robin (*Trillium* species).

Perhaps your rockery is located under trees and receives sunlight only during the early months of spring, before the trees leaf out. In summer, competition for soil moisture is fierce, and the large trees inevitably seem to win. Consider spring ephemerals that carpet the forest floor early in the year with a rush of bloom, then quietly slip into dormancy for the rest of the summer. A walk through the woods in early spring reveals a wealth of native treasures such as rue anemone (*Thalictrum thalictroides*), hepaticas, and bloodroot. These plants are often found growing in the thin soil under large and thirsty deciduous trees on dry, south-facing slopes. Add favorite bulbs such as crocus, snowdrop, and cyclamen, and you will have a lovely display.

BEST AMERICAN
PLANTS FOR

WILDFLOWER
GARDENS

WILDFLOWERS FOR SHADE

by Carole Ottesen

Actaea pachypoda
WHITE BANEBERRY

White baneberry's April flowers, which look like frothy white balls, are followed in late summer and autumn by showy, black-dotted white berries. These fruits have earned the plant another of its common names, doll's eyes. Pretty flowers and intriguing berries add to baneberry's charms, but by far its finest attribute is its graceful, lacy foliage. Baneberry's superb foliage is at once both lush and fine. A boon in the shady garden, it adds freshness and good looks at a time when many early-spring bloomers are fading. Baneberry prefers a slightly acid soil but is otherwise carefree.

White baneberry

NATIVE HABITAT AND RANGE: Woodlands from Nova Scotia, south to Georgia and west to Minnesota and Missouri.

USDA HARDINESS ZONES: 4 to 8

HABIT, USE, AND COMPANIONS: An excellent plant to layer between shrubs and a groundcover such as wild ginger (*Asarum* species), baneberry's handsome 2- to 3-foot-tall foliage adds volume and texture as it camouflages the dying leaves of ephemerals such as Virginia bluebells (*Mertensia virginica*).

CULTIVARS AND RELATED SPECIES: Red baneberry (*A. rubra*) is similar to white baneberry's, but the fruits that emerge in summer are a bright cherry red. The berries of both plants—white and red—are poisonous. Found in woodland and thickets from Labrador to Ontario and south to New Jersey, Pennsylvania, Nebraska, and South Dakota. Zones: 4 to 8.

Aralia racemosa
SPIKENARD

Spikenard's foliage is rugged and striking—big and light green with prominently veined compound leaves. As the plant develops in late spring, there is a sense that something extraordinary is going to happen. Clusters of quiet and respectable greenish-white flowers bloom in early summer, but it isn't until the flowers are followed by stalks of showy purple berries that spring's promise is fulfilled. Spikenard requires shade and moisture to perform at its best.

NATIVE HABITAT AND RANGE: Rich woodlands from Maine to Georgia and west to Minnesota, South Dakota, and Missouri, as well as the Rocky Mountains.

USDA HARDINESS ZONES: 3 to 8

HABIT, USE, AND COMPANIONS: Spikenard grows to 3 feet tall with an equal spread. Its curiously overlapping leaves suggest a cantilevered structure, an unusual habit that draws attention wherever it is placed. It is a bold plant for the back of a woodland border or layering between shrubs and perennials. It also serves as a small specimen shrub and contrasts well with palm branch sedge (*Carex muskingumensis*), hostas, or ferns.

CULTIVARS AND RELATED SPECIES: Wild sarsaparilla (*A. nudicaulis*) is a daintier species than spikenard, growing to 1 to 1½ feet tall with small, green flowers and a pungent aroma. Plant in average to rich, moist soil. Zones 3 to 8.

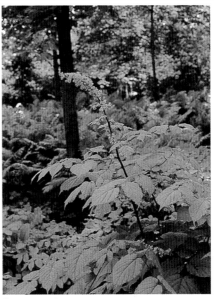

Spikenard

Asarum arifolium
HEARTLEAF WILD GINGER

This ginger's glossy, faintly mottled evergreen leaves are borne on plants that creep outward, but ever so slowly. It stays in place, but grows fuller and more handsome with age as each spring a new flush of shiny bright green leaves appears. For a woodland garden, a groundcover that stays put as this plant does is desirable but hard to find. Lovely and dependable, heartleaf wild ginger is an anchoring plant that frames rambling companions.

NATIVE HABITAT AND RANGE: Rich woodlands from Virginia south to Alabama and Florida.

USDA HARDINESS ZONES: 4 to 9

Heartleaf wild ginger is a bright green groundcover that stays put.

HABIT, USE, AND COMPANIONS: With faintly mottled leaves that spread out, vaselike, from a central clump, heartleaf wild ginger is perfect as an edging plant along a path. At 8 inches tall, it acts as a handsome frame for companions such as fairy wands (*Chamaelirium luteum*) or the taller trilliums like purple toadshade (*Trillium cuneatum*) and yellow trillium (*T. luteum*).

CULTIVARS AND RELATED SPECIES: Also evergreen and roughly similar in appearance but not as hardy is Shuttleworth ginger (*A. shuttleworthii*). It is also far more variable but generally has somewhat rounded, dark green leaves and distinct silver mottling. Varia-tions among the Shuttleworths include wildly mottled gingers, those of more discreet appearance, slow-moving ones, and those that wander ceaselessly. 'Callaway', from Callaway Gardens in Georgia, is an especially fine, vigorous ginger with silver mottling. Found in rich woodlands from Virginia south to Georgia and Alabama. Zones 5 to 8.

Asarum canadense
WILD GINGER

A fast spreader that becomes dense in shade, wild ginger's wonderfully rounded leaves provide intriguing texture and a finished look along edges and paths. A quart-sized pot of wild ginger, planted in moist shade in spring, will easily cover more than a square foot by fall. The only fault of this excellent groundcover is that it is not evergreen like its less hardy counterpart, western wild ginger (*A. caudatum*).

NATIVE HABITAT AND RANGE: Rich woodlands from New Brunswick to North Carolina, west to Missouri.

USDA HARDINESS ZONES: 3 to 8

HABIT, USE, AND COMPANIONS: Wild gingers are great groundcovers and—because they are shallow-rooted—excellent for keeping weeds away from shrubs without competing themselves. It is easy to remove them from places where they are not wanted. They also transplant easily. Because the plants are low—only 6 inches tall—and uniform, they consort beautifully with just about any plant in the garden, but particularly with maidenhair fern (*Adiantum pedatum*), blue phlox (*Phlox divaricata*), and trilliums.

CULTIVARS AND RELATED SPECIES: Western wild ginger (*A. caudatum*) is sometimes called "long-tailed wild ginger" for the long tails on its

Wild ginger, a fast-spreading groundcover, grows densely in shady gardens.

flowers. Like the "little brown jug" flowers of *A. canadense*, these are maroon and brown. One has to get to one's knees and look under the foliage to see them, as they rest directly on the ground, hidden under the leaves. Found in rich woodlands from British Columbia to California. Zones 4 to 8.

Astilbe biternata
FALSE GOATSBEARD

Big and bold, false goatsbeard is one of only two native astilbes. The leaflets of downy green have toothed edges similar to those of the garden-variety (Asian) astilbe—only larger and more rugged looking. Responsive to growing conditions, false goatsbeard will reach a height of 5 feet and bear leaves measuring as much as 2 feet across when grown in the moist, rich soil it prefers.

Rare in the wild, this member of the saxifrage family is unique in the garden. It can be counted upon to provide volume and fullness in the shade, where these attributes are frequently lacking. In comparison to the flowers of garden astilbes, the blooms of false goatsbeard are subdued. In late May and June, pyramid-shaped panicles of small white, yellowish, or cream flowers appear over the top of the leaves.

NATIVE HABITAT AND RANGE: Rich woodlands from Maryland and Virginia south to Georgia, west to Kentucky.

USDA HARDINESS ZONES: 4 to 8

HABIT, USE, AND COMPANIONS: False goatsbeard's grand stature makes it a superb background plant. Strategically planted, a stand of false goatsbeard is a cunning way to stop the eye from wandering out of the garden—or to guide it in the desired direction. Used in numbers, this generous plant can also serve as a loose, informal hedge. As a layering plant, false goatsbeard is just the right size to step down from tall shrubs or understory trees. One layer below false goatsbeard, try goatsbeard (*Aruncus dioicus*) and baneberry (*Actaea* species), which have similar foliage. Better yet, contrast the fine-textured leaves with bold plants such as umbrella leaf (*Diphylleia cymosa*) and wild ginger.

CULTIVARS AND RELATED SPECIES: No other native astilbes available.

Geranium maculatum
WILD GERANIUM

Intoxicating after it has been pelted by raindrops and its leaves release their fragrance, wild geranium ought to be planted where its spicy perfume drifts indoors. Placing a few plants under windows in the

Wild geranium has a spicy fragrance, spreads lustily as it crowds out weeds, and tolerates all light conditions, from deep shade to full sun.

dark spaces between house and shrubs would suit this easy-care plant just fine. This is not to suggest that wild geranium should be hidden from view, however. Its handsome, mounding leaves are a downy green with a hint of mottling. Vibrant pink flowers held over the plants add to its charm.

NATIVE HABITAT AND RANGE: Woodlands and wooded roadsides throughout eastern and central North America.

USDA HARDINESS ZONES: 2 to 8

HABIT, USE, AND COMPANIONS: Growing about 15 inches high, wild geranium forms a low, ground-hugging mound of neat overlapping, deeply incised leaves dotted with bright pink flowers. Planted along edges, wild geranium is reminiscent of a lacy collar. As a groundcover, wild geranium is carefree. It spreads lustily, engulfing shorter weeds. Removal is easy, as wild geranium roots in the top layer of humus and is easier to pull out than it is to transplant. These characteristics make it useful for keeping a garden under control until it is given over to other uses. Wild geranium tolerates virtually any

Round-lobed hepatica seems to arise from nowhere in early spring.

situation from sun to deep shade. It hides the dying after-bloom foliage of bulbs and combines well with tall perennials and ferns such as ostrich fern (*Matteuccia struthiopteris* var. *pensylvanica*) and leggy shrubs such as native azaleas.

CULTIVARS AND RELATED SPECIES: 'Alba' is the name given to white and pale pink selections grown from seed. 'Hazel Gallagher' has large, pure white flowers.

Richardson's geranium (*G. richardsonii*) blooms in early to midsummer. Found in open woods, meadows, and prairies in moist soil in western North America. Zones 4 to 8.

Hepatica nobilis var. *obtusa*
ROUND-LOBED HEPATICA

Sighting the first round-lobed hepatica is one of the rituals of spring. When the first shy flower doffs its fuzzy flower-bud cap to brave wind and weather, winter is officially over. The small blue flowers, some of the daintiest denizens of dry, acid shade, seem to rise out of nowhere—by the time they bloom, their evergreen leaves have often succumbed and disappeared into the ground litter of the previous growing season. Sometimes, when the elements have not totally destroyed them, one can see in round-lobed hepatica's old purple-brown, liver-shaped leaves the reason for one of its common names, liverwort. After the appearance of flowers—which may be blue, white or, less commonly, pink—new fresh, pale green leaves emerge that are also liver-shaped.

NATIVE HABITAT AND RANGE: Nova Scotia, Ontario, Manitoba, and Alaska, south to Georgia, Arkansas, Minnesota, and Iowa.

USDA HARDINESS ZONES: 3 to 8

HABIT, USE, AND COMPANIONS: At less than 6 inches tall, tiny round-lobed hepatica, unless one is lucky enough to have dozens, must be viewed up close to be appreciated. At the edge of a path or, if possible, at eye-level in a terraced garden are the perfect places for it. Excellent companions include other diminutive plants: rue anemone (*Thalictrum thalictroides*), bluets (*Hedyotis* species), and ebony spleenwort (*Asplenium platyneuron*). **CULTIVARS AND RELATED SPECIES:** Sharplobe hepatica (*H. nobilis* var. *acuta*) closely resembles round-lobed hepatica, but its flowers are a bit larger and its leaf blades are pointed. Sharplobe hepatica also grows in a more nearly neutral soil with a pH of 6 to 7. It is found in calcareous woodlands throughout eastern North America. Zones 3 to 8.

Iris cristata
DWARF CRESTED IRIS

This diminutive crested iris, a true dwarf, makes up for what it lacks in stature by lustily fanning out across the ground to form great colonies of bright green, lance-shaped leaves. In this, it behaves like other irises. But where the wildly multiplying garden irises can be too much of a good thing—no matter how attractive their spiky leaves— the small size of crested iris's leaves make it a welcome wanderer.

Crested iris is crowned for much

Dwarf crested iris

too short a time—perhaps a week or so in late April—with exquisitely delicate, purple-blue flowers, crested with orange. Although the flowers are short-lived, if kept moist, the foliage remains through the growing season.

NATIVE HABITAT AND RANGE: Woodlands of Maryland, south to Georgia and west to southern Indiana and Missouri.

USDA HARDINESS ZONES: 3 to 8

HABIT, USE, AND COMPANIONS: Crested iris stands only 6 inches tall with its leaves aligned in the direction of the rhizome from which they arise. It serves

Twinleaf has lovely seedpods and leaves shaped like angel's wings.

admirably as an edging or a low groundcover. It might also be used in a garden of other miniatures, such as the tiny bluets and the round-leaved violet (*Viola rotundifolia*). Other companions of comparable height and contrasting foliage might include creeping phlox (*Phlox stolonifera*) and wood sorrel (*Oxalis acetosella*).

CULTIVARS AND RELATED SPECIES: 'Abby's Violet' has deep purple-blue flowers. 'Shenandoah Skies' has rich, sky-blue flowers. 'Summer Storm' has deep blue flowers. There is also a white-flowered crested iris, *I. cristata* 'Alba'.

Jeffersonia diphylla
TWINLEAF

Too rarely seen in gardens, twinleaf bears starry white flowers that resemble those of bloodroot. One inch across and borne singly on 8-inch stems, the flowers bloom in late April. As pretty as the blossoms are, twinleaf is far more memorable for its unusual leaves. Absolutely unique, these are carried one to a stem with each leaf cleft very nearly in two. Their mirror-image halves give the impression of flat green butterflies. When the wind blows them around, they look like little flags. Their stems continue to grow after the flowers fade until they reach about 15 inches. The seedpods are as unique as the curious leaves. Shaped like tiny tobacco pipes, they have little hinged lids that open when the seeds are ripe.

NATIVE HABITAT AND RANGE: Damp, open woods from Ontario south to Virginia, west to Tennessee, Wisconsin, and Iowa.

USDA HARDINESS ZONES: 3 to 7

HABIT, USE, AND COMPANIONS: Twinleaf's leaves and flowers rise directly from the rootstock and its habit is loose and open, lending it a rather delicate appearance. This looseness is enhanced after flowering, as the stems continue to grow until they mature. Not bothered by insects and seemingly impervious to disease, twinleaf thrives in slightly acid, moist soil. It is an intriguing addition to a woodland border. Its stature and loose habit make it perfect for a position slightly off a path, perhaps behind a patch of creeping phlox or the taller blue phlox (*Phlox divaricata*). Planted with Allegheny spurge (*Pachysandra procumbens*), twinleaf would bloom and rise up over Allegheny spurge before it puts outs its new leaves.

CULTIVARS AND RELATED SPECIES: None available.

Mertensia virginica
VIRGINIA BLUEBELLS

Virginia bluebells grow with wild abandon, popping up everywhere in shady gardens, providing armloads of flowers for picking. Virginia bluebells have been known to spread into dense carpets in the dankest, deepest shade.

The flowers are powder-blue with just a hint of lavender. They appear in April, in clusters of bells that hang suspended above the plants. The leaves are unusual and attractive—broad, smooth, and a pale blue-green with a vague resem-

Virginia bluebells

WILDFLOWERS FOR SHADE

blance to tulip foliage. During the growing season, Virginia bluebells thrive in moist shade, but once they go dormant, a place that becomes dry in summer suits them fine.

NATIVE HABITAT AND RANGE: Moist woods from New York, west to Kansas and south to Alabama.

USDA HARDINESS ZONES: 4 to 8

HABIT, USE, AND COMPANIONS: Upright but relaxed in habit, Virginia bluebells swiftly multiply along running rootstocks and by self-sowing. The mass of spring flowers is wonderfully showy and mixes well with daffodils and early tulips. However, when Virginia bluebells fade, their large leaves turn yellowish cream and are prone to sprawling over neighbors. One must endure their aftermath for the sake of their beauty; plant Virginia bluebells in spots where they will be camouflaged post-bloom by emerging perennials and ferns such as lady fern (*Athyrium filix-femina*).

CULTIVARS AND RELATED SPECIES: Tall lungwort (*M. paniculata*) is a succulent plant from 2 to 3 feet tall with puckered, oval, blue green leaves. The half-inch nodding flowers open in late spring and early summer. Found in open woods and around bogs from Hudson Bay, south to Michigan, Minnesota, and Washington. Zones 4 to 7.

Pachysandra procumbens
ALLEGHENY SPURGE

Allegheny spurge is sometimes called "American pachysandra," and there is a faint family resemblance to that ubiquitous Japanese spurge (*P. terminalis*). Both plants are evergreen where winters are warm. However, unlike its Asian counterpart, Allegheny spurge is not a wildly spreading plant. Rather, it creeps outward at a regular but dignified pace, funneling its energies into growing better and more handsome with age. Its blossoms are a delightful bonus. White and fragrant, the dense flower spikes appear in early spring before the new growth. Resembling textured leather, the new leaves emerge a glowing, solid, bright green. Very slowly, through the long summer and fall, they darken. By winter, they have a silvery variegation that contrasts with their deep, dark green.

NATIVE HABITAT AND RANGE: Kentucky south to Louisiana and Florida.

USDA HARDINESS ZONES: 4 to 7

HABIT, USE, AND COMPANIONS: An outstanding and underused groundcover for partial to full shade, Allegheny spurge is about 1 foot tall and 2 feet in circumference. It is a good edger along paths or in front of bulbs, perennials, and ferns that die down in winter. Solomon's seal

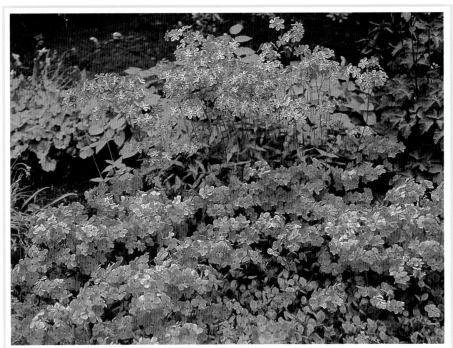

Creeping phlox and its taller relative, blue phlox, carpet the forest floor.

(*Polygonatum biflorum*) is a great companion to arch over Allegheny spurge.

CULTIVARS AND RELATED SPECIES: 'Forest Green' has uniform, shiny green leaves in summer and is much easier to propagate than the species.

Phlox stolonifera
CREEPING PHLOX

A woodland floor alight with the blooms of phlox, like a fantasy spring scene from a Disney cartoon, seems unreal—too good to be true. Yet when creeping phlox carpets a forest floor with flowers, "fairyland" is the first word that comes to mind.

Creeping phlox is a dark green, mat-forming plant whose round leaves disappear under masses of magenta to pink flowers in April. Where winters are warm enough, creeping phlox is evergreen, spreading wherever it isn't shaded out by dense, overhanging plants or heavy leaf litter.

NATIVE HABITAT AND RANGE: Rich woodlands from Pennsylvania to Georgia.

USDA HARDINESS ZONES: 3 to 8

HABIT, USE, AND COMPANIONS: In bloom, creeping phlox stands

Although jacob's ladder looks delicate and fragile, it is a true survivor.

about 6 inches tall. Afterward, its dark green leaves reach barely 2 inches above the ground. It is a fine finishing plant to soften edges or creep around stones. Its foamy blooms are a great foil for upright or arching companions such as purple toadshade or solomon's seal.

CULTIVARS AND RELATED SPECIES: Cultivars include 'Bruce's White' and 'Blue Ridge.' The flowers of blue phlox (*P. divaricata*) are more fragrant than creeping phlox and taller (12 inches). It has narrow, pointed leaves that are not evergreen and makes a good groundcover in wooded areas, where it can flow over competition. Found in rich woodlands from Quebec to Michigan and south to Georgia and Alabama. Zones 3 to 9.

Polemonium reptans
JACOB'S LADDER

In early spring, when the foliage of jacob's ladder first appears, it has a neat, dark green compactness. As the season progresses, its lax stems elongate and, together with its fine, ferny foliage, lend the plant a delicate—almost helpless—appearance. jacob's ladder only looks fragile. It is a true survivor. It is not bothered by insects, needs no winter protection, and returns each spring refreshed and more vigorous. Under the ground, a robust rootstock sends up a steady supply of new green foliage.

After jacob's ladder bears loose groups of dainty blue bell-shaped flowers in late April, the whole plant seems to relax. The long, arching stalks drape themselves over the ground as they begin to form round seed capsules.

NATIVE HABITAT AND RANGE: Open woods and thickets from New York to Kansas, south to Alabama.

USDA HARDINESS ZONES: 3 to 8

HABIT, USE, AND COMPANIONS: Jacob's ladder has long stalks to 20 inches, but they sprawl loosely, making the plant difficult to place and use. Because it prefers a nearly neutral pH of 6 to 7, growing it among rocks or at the edge of a stone or concrete path is a good idea. A little nip here and there with the pruning shears will keep it neat. Too thin by itself to function as groundcover, it serves as a good companion to plants with contrasting and uniform foliage, such as wild ginger or wild stonecrop (*Sedum ternatum*), or with low sedges such as bright apple-green sedge (*Carex austrocaroliniana*).

CULTIVARS AND RELATED SPECIES: 'Blue Pearl' bears a profusion of rich medium-blue flowers, and 'Lambrook Manor' has showy, outward-facing lilac-blue flowers on 2-inch-tall plants.

Sanguinaria canadensis
BLOODROOT

Bloodroot's great charm is a ritual of bloom that begins in March with the emergence of the first tightly rolled leaf, protectively curled around a flower bud. Only when it reaches a safe height does the round, lobed leaf unfurl and release pure white petals around yellow stamens. Bloodroot's flowers can be exceedingly short-lived. An unseasonably hot day will hasten them to maturity so that a stray breeze shatters them. The transience of blossoms adds poignance to the ritual.

The name derives from bloodroot's red sap. It stains, and was once used for dye and war paint.

NATIVE HABITAT AND RANGE: Eastern North America.

USDA HARDINESS ZONES: 3 to 8

HABIT, USE, AND COMPANIONS: Growing only about 10 inches tall but spreading broadly along its rootstalk and by seeds that are carried by ants, bloodroot is best seen close up along a path or in the front of a woodland border.

In the wild, bloodroot grows in colonies, covering lightly wooded, moderately moist slopes. This and bloodroot's tendency to self-sow in the sand between paving stones suggest that it needs good drainage. Dutchman's breeches (*Dicentra cucullaria*), with its frothy, gray-green leaves, and delicate bladder fern (*Cystopteris fragilis*) are good companions that enjoy the same pH of 6 to 7.

CULTIVARS AND RELATED SPECIES: 'Multiplex' produces many-petaled, double white flowers that last longer than the species'.

Stylophorum diphyllum
WOOD POPPY

Wood poppy, also often called celandine poppy, lights up shady gardens with a host of cheerful golden buttercup flowers. Enormously adaptable, wood poppy can grow and bloom anywhere. The gardener should place wood pop-

Wood poppy

pies thoughtfully in the least auspicious sites of the garden and watch them carefully. Their astonishing vigor is a godsend only in places where little else will grow.

Its ornately cut, matte green foliage grows dense and quickly becomes a seamless blanket—a luxuriance in low light conditions.

NATIVE HABITAT AND RANGE: Eastern U.S.

USDA HARDINESS ZONES: 4 to 8

HABIT, USE, AND COMPANIONS: Because of its robust nature and rapid rate of reproduction, wood poppy is best used in places too challenging for other plants to thrive and bloom. The vase-shaped plants grow to 20 inches and shade out lower-growing neighbors, a useful characteristic in establishing a garden in a weedy area, but a hazard for shorter, desirable plants. Young wood poppies are easy to pull up; old ones are not. A watchful eye and a lightning-quick trowel will keep wood poppy in place and away from less robust treasures. Virginia bluebell is one companion that can stand up to wood poppy, if only because Virginia bluebell goes dormant at just about time wood poppy matures.

CULTIVARS AND RELATED SPECIES: None available.

Tellima grandiflora
FRINGECUPS

A native of the Pacific Northwest, fringecups will easily naturalize in partial to full shade as long as it has moist soil. When well sited, it is utterly carefree. At first glance, it's possible to mistake fringecups for foamflowers (*Tiarella* species), a saxifrage relative. Like those of foamflowers, fringecups' leaves grow from a central rosette. They are larger and more hairy—on both the rippled upper and lower surfaces—than most foamflowers' leaves. A heart-shaped outline, cut into rounded lobes on the outside margin of each leaf, gives it a lacy valentine look. Fringecups' leaves are a mottled yellow and green with dark veins that suggest stained glass. In May, yellowish flowers, shaped like tiny fringed cups, bloom along tall, 18-inch stalks.

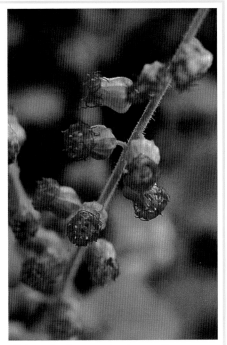

Although the species has yellow flowers, red-flowered cultivars of fringecups are available.

NATIVE HABITAT AND RANGE: Low woodlands of the Pacific Northwest. **USDA HARDINESS ZONES**: 4 to 9 **HABIT, USE, AND COMPANIONS**: Fringecups stand about 6 inches high but radiate out a foot from their central rosettes. When happily situated, the plant produces new plants by runners and by seed. It is adaptable, accommodating, generally pest-free, and, thanks to its hirsutism, seems to be slug-proof. A few plants are a pleasant accent along a woodland path. As a groundcover, fringecups won't spread evenly. The cunning gardener can fill vacant spaces with ferns and trilliums. As an edging, the plant's rounded leaves give it a formal look. Its understated yellow variegation makes it a good companion to the mountain male fern (*Dryopteris oreades*), yellow *Acorus* species, and variegated hostas.

CULTIVARS AND RELATED SPECIES: 'Perky' has smaller leaves than the species and red flowers.

Foamflower

Tiarella cordifolia
FOAMFLOWER

The frothy drifts of white that grace woodlands in the spring are courtesy of the plant whose common name is particularly apt: foamflower. On each plant, flower stalks held above the leaves are composed of dozens of tiny white blossoms. One rarely sees a single foamflower. This plant rambles through woodland along far-reaching stolons (stems that run along the ground, forming new plants) to create large, free-form drifts. Foamflower's leaves—generally lobed, variegated, and heart-shaped—are as lovely as its flowers.

NATIVE HABITAT AND RANGE: Moist woods from Nova Scotia and Ontario south to Georgia and west to Indiana, Michigan, and Minnesota.

USDA HARDINESS ZONES: 4 to 8

HABIT, USE, AND COMPANIONS: Foamflower's leaves radiate out from a central rosette about 6 inches tall (the plant is a foot tall when in flower in April or May). A classic woodland groundcover, foamflower thrives in a moist and moderately acid to neutral soil and blooms in fairly dense shade. It is pretty with false solomon's seal (*Maianthemum racemosum*) and clumpers like the Christmas fern (*Polystichum acrostichoides*).

CULTIVARS AND RELATED SPECIES: In recent years, the variability of the leaves has inspired nurserymen to produce a bewildering array of cultivars and selections. 'Eco Running Tapestry', 'Filigree Lace', and 'Oakleaf' are some of these, and their names say it all. Some of the foamflowers now available commercially include nonrunning types that stay put.

Trillium cuneatum
PURPLE TOADSHADE

In addition to purple toadshade, this wildflower has been called whippoorwill flower, bloody butcher, and sweet betsy. The host of common names with conflicting connotations is not surprising. This is a trillium to be reckoned with— an early-spring-blooming, big, bold trillium of darkly organic coloring.

It is the largest sessile (meaning the flower, having no "neck," sits directly upon the leaves) trillium in the East, standing up to 20 inches tall. Three substantial leaves, often marbled gray, spread out stiffly, framing the flower. The long-lasting flowers hold their three petals upright. The petals are often maroon but may be yellow, chartreuse, or bronze. Some smell good, like a faint whiff of sweet shrub (*Calycanthus* species), while others have an unpleasant odor.

One of the easiest trilliums to grow, purple toadshade doesn't take long to form a large colony. When it does, the effect is spectacular. In the wild, purple toadshade grows most magnificently on limestone or shale bluffs and favors sloping sites.

NATIVE HABITAT AND RANGE: Rich, upland woods of southern Kentucky, Tennessee west of the Appalachians; North Carolina, east of the mountains, and south to Mississippi and Alabama.

USDA HARDINESS ZONES: 5 to 8

A yellow form of purple toadshade

HABIT, USE, AND COMPANIONS: Purple toadshade can hold its own a little back from a path or front of a woodland border. Its height allows it to share a space with lower-growing plants such as wood phlox, wild gingers, or Allegheny spurge.

CULTIVARS AND RELATED SPECIES: Prairie trillium (*T. recurvatum*) is also sessile but has smaller leaves and red-brown flowers. Yellow trillium (*T. luteum*) has chartreuse to lemon-yellow flowers.

Trillium grandiflorum
GREAT WHITE TRILLIUM

Trilliums have always seemed to possess a magical aura. In the past they were deemed too untamed for the cultivated garden. While it is indeed an amazing flower to come upon in the wilderness, the great white trillium is also a hardy, care-

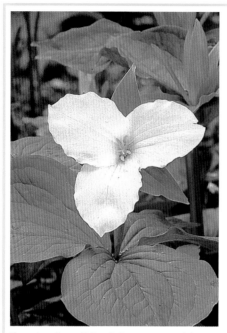

Despite its wild origins, great white trillium is carefree in the garden.

mature. The leaves are a clean, unmottled green. As the plant ages, it tends to clump rather than spread singly, as do some other trilliums, making it more striking with each passing year.

NATIVE HABITAT AND RANGE: Open woods and slopes from Quebec to Ontario and south to North Carolina, Missouri, and Minnesota.

USDA HARDINESS ZONES: 3 to 8

HABIT, USE, AND COMPANIONS: Older plants that have spread wider than their height of about 18 inches look like low-growing shrubs. This shrubby habit is especially pleasing when the plant is grown among rocks. The dwarf lady fern (*Athyrium filix-femina* 'Minutissimum'), which grows a feathery 12 inches tall, is a splendid companion. Later on, when the great white trillium dies down in summer, its vacated space may be filled with the fall-blooming white wood aster (*Eurybia divaricata*).

CULTIVARS AND RELATED SPECIES: Snow trillium (*T. nivale*) is a small plant with egg-shaped, gray-green leaves and tiny snow-white flowers in earliest spring. Found in rich, rocky deciduous woods, on outcroppings, and river bluffs from Pennsylvania and Minnesota, south to West Virginia and Nebraska. Zones 4 to 8.

free garden plant. If there is any mystery surrounding it, it is that of origin. Because it takes about seven years from seed to flower, many of the trilliums sold have been dug out of our national parklands. Taking care to buy trilliums that have been nursery propagated from reliable sources will ensure that you have acquired a healthy plant without contributing to the depletion of trilliums in the wild.

An excellent plant for the woodland garden, the great white trillium blooms for a full month—usually late April into May, its flowers turning from white to rosy pink as they

Uvularia grandiflora
GREAT MERRYBELLS

After a year or two in the ground, great merrybells begin to form fine colonies that are a welcome sight in the spring garden. Their foliage is arresting: elegantly arching, forking stalks clasped by long, cascading green leaves. Among the leaves are dangling bell flowers, echoing the long shape of the leaves. They are also often called "large-flowered bellwort."

Each bloom is a lovely corn yellow with a hint of green, only a few shades removed from the pale green of the foliage. In the generally subdued world of woodland plants, great merrybells are more quietly elegant than most, yet they never fail to draw attention. They disappear in summer.

Great merrybells

NATIVE HABITAT AND RANGE: Moist slopes in woodlands from Quebec to Ontario and south to Georgia, Kansas, and Minnesota.

USDA HARDINESS ZONES: 3 to 8

HABIT, USE, AND COMPANIONS: A well-grown colony of great merrybells reaches 2 feet tall and at least as wide as it spreads by rhizomes through moist, humus-rich soil. Its pale color and strongly cascading habit contrast with just about all of its neighbors and make it an intriguing focus. It is spectacular in combination with maidenhair fern and wild ginger (*Asarum canadense*), with its dark, leathery, orbicular leaves. Allegheny spurge is a good groundcover nearby.

CULTIVARS AND RELATED SPECIES: Wild oats (*U. sessilifolia*) is a delicate, running plant with sessile, oval leaves and nodding, straw-colored flowers. Plants weave in and out among ferns and other wildflowers in the spring garden. 'Variegata' has showy leaves with creamy-white margins. Found in acidic woods from New England, west to North Dakota, and south in the mountains to South Carolina and Arkansas. Zones 3 to 8.

WILDFLOWERS FOR PARTIAL SHADE

by Kim Hawks

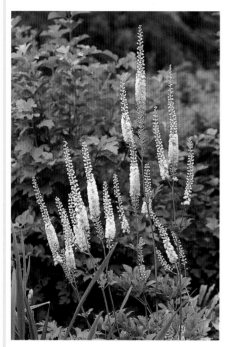

Black cohosh

Actaea (formerly *Cimicifuga*) *racemosa*
BLACK COHOSH, BUGBANE

This audacious wildflower commands attention as its pure white flowering spikes reach 6 to 8 feet, creating a candelabrum of light in shady areas. The plant's strong odor is believed to repel bugs (hence the common name bugbane)—all the more reason to cultivate it.

Black cohosh thrives in moist, humusy, rich soil. Though is is a bit slow to become established and fill out, the patient gardener will be rewarded with its beauty. Plant it where it will not be touched by harsh afternoon sun. Despite its tall stature, it does not require staking.

NATIVE HABITAT AND RANGE: Rich woods and clearings from southern Ontario, Massachusetts, south to Georgia, and west to Tennessee and Missouri.

USDA HARDINESS ZONES: 3 to 8

HABIT, USE, AND COMPANIONS: Large, compound, sharply serrated leaves bear vertical, leafy stalks of white flowers in early summer. The white, spiked blossoms can accent the white- and pink-tinged fronds of Japanese painted ferns (*Athyrium niponicum* var. *pictum*) or the contrasting foliage of hostas, especially plants with white variegation. Great blue lobelia echoes black cohosh's tall spikes.

CULTIVARS AND RELATED SPECIES: The southeastern U.S. species Kearney's bugbane (*A. rubifolia*) complements cool, moist woodland gardens with its slender, wandlike racemes of white.

Amsonia hubrichtii
HUBRICHT'S BLUESTAR

I'm in love with this particular bluestar. It has everything going for it: wonderful, needlelike foliage; numerous star-shaped, steel-blue flowers in early spring; and foliage that turns banana yellow in the fall before going dormant. I expect fall color from many of our native trees and shrubs in the fall, but from a perennial? That is indeed unusual.

This tough native handles dry or well-drained, partial-shade conditions with ease. It basks in bright or all-morning sunlight. Although it has a restricted native habitat, it is very adaptable in the cultivated garden.

NATIVE HABITAT AND RANGE: Along creeks and streambanks in west-central Arkansas and Oklahoma.

USDA HARDINESS ZONES: 4 to 9

HABIT, USE, AND COMPANIONS: Over time Hubricht's bluestar makes a striking statement with a soft, rounded form, topping out at 3 to 4 feet with an equal spread. At the Chanticleer gardens in Pennsylvania they are planted en masse in a circular parking lot island. I saw them one week before the peak fall color, and they were stunning. The

Hubricht's bluestar

fine texture contrasts nicely with the bold foliage of hostas (especially 'Love Pat', with its blue cupped leaves) or American alumroot (*Heuchera americana*), particularly 'Pewter Veil'.

CULTIVARS AND RELATED SPECIES: The flowers of willow bluestar (*A. tabernaemontana*) are, like Hubricht's, star-shaped and steel blue. However, the leaves of willow bluestar are lance-shaped like weeping willow's. It has a loose, round form to 3 to 4 feet.

Aquilegia canadensis
EASTERN WILD COLUMBINE

Upward-pointing, deep coral-red spurs with lemon-yellow petals appear in early spring. Deep within these bell-shaped, tubular flowers, nectar waits to be sipped by early-migrating hummingbirds. The

Eastern wild columbine

HABIT, USE, AND COMPANIONS: This is one of the few eastern native plants with bright coral-red flowers. It contrasts well with the floating blue flowers of blue phlox (*Phlox divaricata*), or echoes the butter-yellow blossoms of celandine poppy (*Stylophorum diphyllum*). **CULTIVARS AND RELATED SPECIES:** 'Corbett' is shorter than the species, with soft primrose-yellow flowers. Western wild columbine (*A. formosa*) is the western U.S. version of eastern wild columbine, with similar flowers of bright yellow and red spurs atop 3-foot plants. Flowering occurs in late spring through early summer.

flowers emerge from 3-foot stalks atop a loose mound of compound, trilobed leaflets.

Eastern wild columbine detests poorly drained areas but will give years of beauty in open shade, where it may naturalize by seeding in. If this is not desired, simply remove the flowering stalks just below the foliage as soon as the flowers fade. **NATIVE HABITAT AND RANGE:** Rocky, wooded, or open slopes from Ontario to Quebec; south through New England to Florida and Texas; west to Tennessee and Wisconsin. **USDA HARDINESS ZONES:** 2 to 8

Aruncus dioicus
GOATSBEARD

This is a bold plant when in bloom, in early summer, as 6-foot leafstalks of compound leaflets push forth graceful pure white plumes of frothy flowers.

Bright, diffuse light and moist, rich soil keep goatsbeard in heavy bloom. In deep shade, blooms are sparse, but this wildflower tolerates full sun if sited in a consistently moist soil. **NATIVE HABITAT AND RANGE:** Pennsylvania south to Georgia, west to Alabama, Kentucky, Arkansas, and Pacific Northwest.

USDA HARDINESS ZONES: 3 to 8
HABIT, USE, AND COMPANIONS:
Plant goatsbeard as a backdrop to
woodland ferns, native alumroot,
wild bleeding heart (*Dicentra
eximia*), and hostas, or let it pop up
through low groundcovers such as
green-and-gold (*Chrysogonum
virginianum*), carpet bugleweed
(*Ajuga reptans*), or perennial geranium species. Plants are either
male or female, but because the
male flowers are showier, most
nurseries offer only male plants. A
male or female plant is worth having in the garden for early-summer
color.

CULTIVARS AND RELATED SPECIES:
None widely available.

Caltha palustris
MARSH MARIGOLD

Shiny, butter-yellow flowers cluster
among wavy, heart-shaped leaves
rising from thick, hollow, branching
stems. Marsh marigold is a short
wetland plant of 5 to 7 inches whose
flowers resemble buttercups rather
than marigolds. It adds springtime
color to boggy areas that get bright
or diffused sun, then goes dormant
in summer.
NATIVE HABITAT AND RANGE:
Swamps, marshes, wet meadows,

WILDFLOWERS FOR
PARTIAL SHADE

Marsh marigold brings bright splashes of color to wetlands or bog areas.

Pink turtlehead

'Alba' is a robust cultivar with white flowers that bloom for up to a month. 'Flore Pleno', also sold as 'Multiplex', is a fast-growing selection with double flowers.

Chelone lyonii
PINK TURTLEHEAD

Pink turtlehead is a late-summer-blooming native for light shade. The distinctive reddish-purple flowers nestle atop colonies of 3- to 4-foot-tall stems. The flower's shape and a spot of purple make it resemble a turtle's head. Pink turtlehead is versatile, tolerating well-drained sites as well as poorly drained areas. The wetter the site, the more sun it can take.

NATIVE HABITAT AND RANGE: Moist areas in clearings or diffuse light in the southern Appalachian Mountains of North Carolina, South Carolina, Georgia, and Tennessee.

USDA HARDINESS ZONES: 3 to 8

HABIT, USE, AND COMPANIONS: Although it tolerates dry soils, pink turtlehead is happiest in moist, poorly drained areas. In well-drained areas, pink turtlehead pops up through 'Burgundy Glow' carpet bugleweed or coexists easily with deadnettles (*Lamium maculatum* 'Beedham's White' or 'Beacon Silver'). In poorly drained areas, plant

pond edges, and streambanks in boreal areas of North America, south to North Carolina, west to Iowa and Nebraska and into Alaska.

USDA HARDINESS ZONES: 2 to 8

HABIT, USE, AND COMPANIONS: Marsh marigold dapples soggy landscapes with tight clumps of sunny yellow. For stunning wetland compositions, add some pickerel weed (*Pontederia cordata*) to provide a contrast of foot-long vertical spikes of blue, or the grassy clumps of white-bracted sedge (*Rhynchospora latifolia*), with its showy, pure white flowers dipped in green.

with woodland ferns, blue flag iris (*Iris versicolor*), or great blue lobelia (*Lobelia siphilitica*).

CULTIVARS AND RELATED SPECIES: Smooth turtlehead (*C. glabra*) has lance-shaped leaves and white flowers tinted with purple. Plants form open clumps with 2- to 4-foot stalks. Found in wetlands and low meadows from Newfoundland and Georgia, west to Minnesota and Alabama. Zones 3 to 8.

Darmera peltata
UMBRELLA PLANT

In early spring, large glistening leaves pop open like umbrellas behind clusters of starry pink flowers. Although the 2-foot-tall flowers are not showy, the plants give a lush, tropical look to wet areas.

Though it grows in shady bogs, the wetter the site, the more sun it tolerates. Umbrella plant is also at home in dense, wet clay, where few plants volunteer to live.

NATIVE HABITAT AND RANGE: Mountain streams from southern Oregon to northern Canada.

USDA HARDINESS ZONES: 4 to 8

HABIT, USE, AND COMPANIONS: Anchor corners of water gardens with a showy mound of umbrella foliage, or plant where the low angle of light at sunrise and sunset can filter through the 18- to 24-inch

Umbrella plant

leaves. Give it plenty of room, whether it is alone or in the company of other robust, moisture-loving plants, such as southern blue flag iris (*Iris virginica*).

CULTIVARS AND RELATED SPECIES: None available.

Dicentra eximia
WILD BLEEDING HEART

Delicate fernlike foliage subtly tinted blue-green and tiny nodding pink flowers throughout spring and sporadically during the summer make this an indispensable plant for the woodland garden. Grow in humus-

WILDFLOWERS FOR PARTIAL SHADE

Wild bleeding heart

ginger; the subtle white mottling of Allegheny spurge (*Pachysandra procumbens*); or the delicate spikes of foamflower (*Tiarella cordifolia*).

CULTIVARS AND RELATED SPECIES: Western bleeding heart (*D. formosa*) is similar to its eastern cousin in leaf and flower, though the blossoms are larger and it has a spreading rather than clumping habit. Although it is native to the western U.S., it can be grown successfully elsewhere given bright, diffuse light.

Eurybia divaricata (formerly *Aster divaricatus*)
WHITE WOOD ASTER

This quietly charming plant is happy in the shade and blooms from late summer through early fall. It is easy to grow; select a spot in diffused light with moisture-retentive soil that is enriched with organic matter. White wood aster is tolerant of dry summertime spells. The small but numerous flowers have single petals with yellow centers that brighten up shade gardens. Black, twiggy stems provide a showy contrast to white flowers. As the season passes, the flowers turn a subtle burgundy and rosy pink.

NATIVE HABITAT AND RANGE: Dry, open woods from New England to Ohio, south to Georgia and Alabama.

rich, moist yet well-drained soil; avoid soggy areas. Bright, diffuse light is best.

NATIVE HABITAT AND RANGE: Open woods from southwestern Pennsylvania southward to Tennessee and North Carolina.

USDA HARDINESS ZONES: 3 to 9

HABIT, USE, AND COMPANIONS: Softly rounded mounds of feathery foliage 18 inches high nestle comfortably near the front of the border. Clustered, heart-shaped flowers open along stems that pop up through the foliage and gently arch over. Wild bleeding heart constrasts well with the fans of dwarf crested iris (*Iris cristata*); the smooth, heart-shaped leaves of wild

USDA HARDINESS ZONES: 3 to 8

HABIT, USE, AND COMPANIONS:
Whether planted in masses or placed here and there as highlights, white wood aster is a must in the shade garden. It carpets the earth with flowers like snowflakes. It has a casual, loose, sprawling habit, forming a 1- to 2-foot groundcover of arrow-shaped, serrated leaves. White wood aster looks great just behind American alumroot or near the purple-spotted, late-summer flowers of toad lily (*Tricyrtis* species). Or, plant white wood aster as a carpet beneath woodland trees, such as sweet bay magnolia (*Magnolia virginiana*) or eastern redbud (*Cercis canadensis*).

CULTIVARS AND RELATED SPECIES:
Symphyotrichum cordifolium (formerly *Aster cordifolius*) is a bit larger, to 3 feet, with heart-shaped leaves and sky-blue to white flowers. 'Little Caro' has mounds of sky-blue flowers on 2-foot plants. Native to open woods from Nova Scotia and Georgia, west to Minnesota and Missouri. Zones 4 to 8.

Gillenia trifoliatus
BOWMAN'S ROOT
Starry, ethereal flowers on wiry, branched stems add an airy feel to the woodland garden. Bowman's root thrives in dappled or open sun

as long as the harsh afternoon sunlight is avoided. Plant in well-drained, acidic soil.

NATIVE HABITAT AND RANGE:
Wooded uplands of northeastern U.S. and Canada.

USDA HARDINESS ZONES: 4 to 8

HABIT, USE, AND COMPANIONS:
Equally at home in the herbaceous border or the woodland garden, bowman's root plays a supporting role to other showy perennials. Bright white to pinkish-white flowers perched on mahogany stems lighten up the summer shade garden. Other pleasing companions are the small- to medium-leaved hostas, the heart-shaped leaves of American alumroot, and woodland ferns.

CULTIVARS AND RELATED SPECIES:
American ipecac (*G. stipulatus*) is similar but has a more open habit. The leaves are deeply toothed, and the petioles bear persistent stipules that give the plant a winged look. Found in open woods from New York and Georgia, west to Illinois and Texas. Zones 4 to 9.

Heuchera americana
AMERICAN ALUMROOT
This plant has lovely tiny green flowers, but its beautiful foliage is its strongest trait. American alumroot's leaves are green and

WILDFLOWERS FOR PARTIAL SHADE

burgundy with shiny silver high-lights. Scalloped, heart-shaped leaves form full 1- to 2-foot mounds that coexist happily with many other woodland treasures.

American alumroot grows effort-lessly in woodsy soil enriched with leaf mold or compost, in diffuse or bright light. Pick a spot with after-noon shade and you'll be rewarded with colorful foliage summer through frost.

NATIVE HABITAT AND RANGE: In woods, shady slopes, and rocky outcroppings from Ontario, New England, and Michigan, south to Georgia, west to Alabama, and into Oklahoma.

USDA HARDINESS ZONES: 4 to 9
HABIT, USE, AND COMPANIONS: Olive-green or burgundy, almost leafless stems push up 2-foot flow-ering stalks of tiered, tiny apple-green buds that become greenish flowers. Pleasing combi-nations are endless. To play off the burgundy colors in late summer, plant American alumroot in front of carpet bugleweed (*Ajuga reptans* 'Burgundy Glow'), a variegated pink groundcover; the white and pink fronds of Japanese painted fern; or pink turtlehead. Blue star creeper (*Isotoma fluviatilis*) has tight, ground-hugging foliage and powder-blue flowers could weave

around the base of American alum-root. Great blue lobelia's summertime spikes bring out the subtle blue in American alumroot's foliage. Two native sedge species, *Carex eburnea* and *C. pensylvanica*, offer contrasting, grassy foliage to nestle near American alumroot.

CULTIVARS AND RELATED SPECIES: Thanks to the breeding work of Dan Heims and several other noted growers, there are numerous culti-vars available to today's gardeners; most offer slightly different variega-tions, though work is being done to produce showier flowers. Hairy alumroot (*H. villosa*) is another fabu-lous southeastern native with hairy stems and round, lobed leaves, com-plete with showy panicles of creamy white flowers in late summer. En masse, it is a showstopper and fur-ther extends the alumroot season.

Iris virginica
SOUTHERN BLUE FLAG IRIS
Hard to find in the trade, this is a knock-out iris with strong, fat, verti-cal fans that arch over at the tips and bear early summer flowers of violet-blue splotched with yellow. Native to wetlands, find a poorly drained or frequently damp spot (everybody has a ditch!) and you'll be rewarded with its beauty and ease of growth.

Southern blue flag iris is a bold, tall wildflower that likes to have wet feet.

NATIVE HABITAT AND RANGE:
Wetlands from Virginia to Florida and Texas.

USDA HARDINESS ZONES: 7 to 8

HABIT, USE, AND COMPANIONS:
This is a vigorous iris with bold, dense, 4-foot foliage that provides a strong vertical accent in the partial-shade to full-sun garden. Find a wet site, perhaps next to a pond, near pickerel weed, or in front of the pure white, early-summer spires of Virginia sweetspire (*Itea virginica*). Southern blue flag iris also thrives in moist yet well-drained sites with a myriad of pleasing companions, including prairie phlox (*Phlox pilosa*), sundrop (*Oenothera fruticosa*), or showy primrose (*Oenothera speciosa*). It looks great popping through the sunshine-yellow foliage of the groundcover, golden creeping jenny (*Lysimachia nummularia* 'Aurea').

CULTIVARS AND RELATED SPECIES:
Blue flag iris (*I. versicolor*) is similar, although its swordlike foliage tops out at 2 to 3 feet, and it has slightly smaller flowers and a yellow-based sepal. Its culture is the same as southern blue flag iris.

Lobelia cardinalis
CARDINAL FLOWER
In Chapel Hill, North Carolina, Labor Day is ushered in with the 3- to 4-foot spikes of blood-red car-

dinal flower. Hummingbirds love cardinal flower, and it thrives in moist, lightly shaded areas, such as along streams. In autumn, remove any fallen tree leaves around the plants, as the rosettes need the winter sun to survive. Allow the plants to go to seed; eventually, you'll be rewarded with a dense colony of brilliant red in late summer.

NATIVE HABITAT AND RANGE: Low meadows and alongside creeks from southern Ontario and Quebec to New Brunswick and Minnesota, south to Florida, and west to eastern Texas.

Cardinal flower

USDA HARDINESS ZONES: 2 to 9

HABIT, USE, AND COMPANIONS: From flat rosettes rise multiple flowering spikes that bear numerous tubular, bright red flowers. Small, five-petaled flowers are intricate, comprising two upper lips and three lower lips. Plant at the back of a wet area with native ferns in the foreground and some Virginia spiderwort (*Tradescantia virginiana*) nearby. The flowers of white turtlehead (*Chelone glabra*) contrast nicely with the intense red of cardinal flower.

CULTIVARS AND RELATED SPECIES: While the tubular flower is similar to cardinal flower's, great blue lobelia (*Lobelia siphilitica*) bears shorter multiple spikes of 2- to 3-foot blue flowers in late summer. It also tolerates a dryer site and more sun than cardinal flower, residing happily in a lightly shaded garden with moist yet well-drained soil.

Lysichiton americanus
WESTERN SKUNK CABBAGE

Dramatic, late-winter flowers and bold foliage make this an eye-catching native for soggy woodland areas. Skunk cabbage thrives where most other plants fail, in partially shady spots with poor drainage. Its common name comes from the musky odor of both the flowers and foliage, but it is not overly offensive and should not deter gardeners from growing this great wetland native.

NATIVE HABITAT AND RANGE: Wetlands, swamps, and wet woodlands in western North America.

USDA HARDINESS ZONES: 7 to 9

HABIT, USE, AND COMPANIONS: Gardeners are rewarded with a jump on spring when open ovate yellow sheathes surrounding a vertical green flower appear in late winter. The curious yet showy flowers bloom without foliage and, although the 2-foot flowers hover near the ground, they are quite noticeable, since the surrounding woodland is still dormant and not visible. After flowering, lush, glossy leaves claim their space, choking out even the most persistent weeds. Plant cardinal flower close by to provide color at the end of the season. Ferns provide a pleasing contrast.

CULTIVARS AND RELATED SPECIES: None available.

Maianthemum racemosum
FALSE SOLOMON'S SEAL

Burnt-orange berries with purple spots hang at the ends of arching 2- to 3-foot stalks and light up the woodland garden in fall. Grow false

Western skunk cabbage

solomon's seal in dappled shade in soil rich in organic matter with good drainage.

NATIVE HABITAT AND RANGE: Woodland areas from Nova Scotia and British Columbia, south to Georgia, west to Arizona and California.

USDA HARDINESS ZONES: 3 to 8

HABIT, USE, AND COMPANIONS: False solomon's seal is highly adaptable to a variety of locations in the woodland garden. The satiny foliage bears fluffy white terminal flower spikes in spring and combines beautifully with ferns, wild bleeding heart, and Japanese roof iris (*Iris tectorum*). In the fall, when the distinctive berries of false

Chattahoochee phlox

Virginia, west to British Columbia and California. Zones 2 to 8.

Phlox 'Chattahoochee'
CHATTAHOOCHEE PHLOX

This native groundcover cultivar has periwinkle-blue, five-petaled flowers and an enchanting maroon eye and is at home in many places in the springtime garden. Although Chattahoochee phlox seems to detest growing in a pot and looks insignificant at the nursery, it fills out nicely if you plant it in a spot that receives half a day of direct sun to bright filtered sunlight. After flowering, cut back to help it tighten up.
NATIVE HABITAT AND RANGE: The species that are crossed in this hybrid occur throughout the U.S.
USDA HARDINESS ZONES: 4 to 8
HABIT, USE, AND COMPANIONS: This sprawling phlox provides a pleasing carpet under the pinkish purple, tulip-shaped flowers of saucer magnolia (*Magnolia* × *soulangeana*)—the maroon eye matches the magnolias. Intermingle it with blue muscari or carpet bugleweed 'Jungle Beauty', or plant it beneath the delicate blossoms of pink loropetalum (*Loropetalum chinensis* f. *rubrum*).
CULTIVARS AND RELATED SPECIES: Wild blue phlox (*P. divaricata*) is a parent of 'Chattahoochee', with soft

solomon's seal appear in clusters at the end of the stems, the bronzy foliage of autumn fern (*Dryopteris erythrosora*) makes a stunning combination.
CULTIVARS AND RELATED SPECIES: Starry solomon's plume (*M. stellatum*) is a delicate plant with lance-shaped to narrow oval, blue-green leaves and small clusters of starry white flowers. The showy berries are bright green with red stripes. Plants grow in sun or shade in rich soil. Found in woods and on prairies from Newfoundland and

sky-blue flowers and a heavenly scent. The oval, evergreen leaves form an open groundcover. Plants reseed freely and create lovely drifts. There are many named selections in a range of colors, including white. Found in open woods and flood plains from Quebec and Georgia, west to Minnesota and Texas. Zones 3 to 9.

Phlox maculata
WILD SWEET WILLIAM

Considered a mainstay for herbaceous borders in partial shade or full sun, this 2- to 3-foot phlox presents rounded heads of mauve-pink flowers in early summer. Because of its short stature, it is an excellent choice for smaller gardens. Grow in soil amended with organic matter. Wild sweet william tolerates slightly damp sites as well as well-drained areas.

NATIVE HABITAT AND RANGE: Moist roadsides in Virginia, Georgia, Tennessee, Kentucky, and West Virginia

USDA HARDINESS ZONES: 3 to 8

HABIT, USE, AND COMPANIONS: Plant near the front to the middle of the border in full sun or open, diffused light. Wild sweet william goes well with other early-summer-

WILDFLOWERS FOR PARTIAL SHADE

Wild sweet william, available in pale hues as well as bright ones, like 'Alpha', is excellent for smaller gardens, since it never grows very tall.

blooming perennials, such as double Japanese aster (*Kalimeris pinnatifida*), with creamy-white flowers, or shasta daisy 'Becky' (*Leucanthemum × superbum* 'Becky'). Accent with the burgundy color and contrasting, feathery foliage of bronze fennel (*Foeniculum vulgare* 'Purpureum'). Grow dwarf or compact daylilies or creeping verbena (*Verbena canadensis*) at the feet of wild sweet william.

CULTIVARS AND RELATED SPECIES: Numerous cultivars are available, selected for traits such as powdery mildew resistance and colors such as pure white, to white with a purple eye to rosy pink.

Solidago flexicaulis
ZIGZAG GOLDENROD

This zigzag-stemmed goldenrod blooms in summer and is easy to grow in open shade or a lightly shaded woodland border.

NATIVE HABITAT AND RANGE: Moist, open woods in eastern North America.

USDA HARDINESS ZONES: 4 to 8

HABIT, USE, AND COMPANIONS: Sharply toothed, egg-shaped leaves bear short clusters of flowers in the leaf axils or in a terminal cluster. The zigzagged stem gives a slightly angled appearance on this 2- to 3-foot goldenrod, complementing the predominantly green textures in the woodland garden. Zigzag goldenrod provides a pleasing canopy over partridge berry (*Mitchella repens*), green-and-gold, or creeping woodland phlox (*Phlox stolonifera*). Place some great blue lobelia nearby to offer contrasting 3-foot blue spikes.

CULTIVARS AND RELATED SPECIES: Wreath goldenrod (*S. caesia*) has narrow blue-green leaves mingling along the stem with spikes of yellow flowers. Found in open woods and clearings throughout eastern North America. Zones 4 to 9.

Spigelia marilandica
INDIAN PINK

People are intrigued by the unusual flowers of this woodland plant. Indian pink grows unnoticed until midsummer, when bright-lipstick-red trumpet-shaped blossoms open to reveal greenish-yellow starlike flowers that face skyward. Indian pink prefers dappled shade in well-drained soils with organic matter.

NATIVE HABITAT AND RANGE: Open woodlands and streambanks from Maryland south to Florida; west to Texas, Missouri, and Oklahoma.

USDA HARDINESS ZONES: 4 to 9

HABIT, USE, AND COMPANIONS: Because of its small stature of 2 to 3 feet, plant Indian pink near a pathway where you can admire the detail of the flowers. Plants with chartreuse foliage that dwell in the shade make stunning combinations, such as small- to medium-leaved chartreuse hostas or golden club moss (*Selaginella kraussiana* 'Aurea').

CULTIVARS AND RELATED SPECIES: None available.

Thalictrum thalictroides
RUE ANEMONE

"Drought tolerant" and "delicate yet tough" are the first descriptions that come to mind for this diminutive, spring-blooming native. The round, lobed leaflets of rue anemone offset its numerous tiny flowers in shades of white, soft pink, or medium pink, which gently float above the foliage.

Bright, diffuse light suits this anemone, yielding more flowers and tighter foliage. In summer drought, rue anemone may go dormant, but it faithfully returns the following spring.

NATIVE HABITAT AND RANGE: In open woods from southwest Maine to northwest Florida; west to Alabama, Mississippi, Arkansas, and Oklahoma; north to Minnesota.

USDA HARDINESS ZONES: 3 to 8

Plant Indian pink near a pathway in dappled sunlight to enjoy its delicate, brightly colored flowers.

HABIT, USE, AND COMPANIONS: This delicate beauty only 4 to 8 inches tall deserves front-row placement alongside dwarf crested iris (*Iris cristata*), wild gingers (*Asarum* species), or ground-hugging partridge berry (*Mitchella repens*).

CULTIVARS AND RELATED SPECIES: 'Betty Blake' has apple-green double flowers and blooms for nearly a month. 'Cameo' is a soft pink double. "Shoaff's Double Pink' is a rich, rosy pink.

WILDFLOWERS FOR SUN

by C. Colston Burrell

Baptisia alba, B. lactea, B. leucantha, and B. pendula
WHITE WILD INDIGO

Wild indigos are handsome perennials with colorful spikes of pealike flowers in blue, yellow, cream, and white. The flowers look like those of lupines, but the habit is quite different. Plants are 2 to 5 feet tall, with trilobed, sea-green leaves. The inflated brown seedpods nod in open clusters through the autumn.

Wild indigos thrive on neglect. Plant them in rich, moist but well-drained soils in full sun or light shade. All species are drought tolerant once established. Wild indigos are slow to establish, but in time they spread to form huge clumps. Space individual plants at least 3 feet apart, as they are difficult to move once the taproot gets established.

NATIVE HABITAT AND RANGE: Open woods, meadows, prairie, and savannas in moist or dry soils from Ontario and Minnesota, south to Florida and Texas.

USDA HARDINESS ZONES: 4 to 8

HABIT, USE, AND COMPANIONS: The tall, white-flowered spikes of wild white indigo are held above dense foliage mounds in late spring and early summer. Use them in meadow and prairie gardens with fire pinks (*Silene virginica*), butterfly weed (*Asclepias tuberosa*), bowman's-root (*Gillenia trifoliata*), and prairie phlox (*Phlox pilosa*). Indigos are dramatic border plants. Use them as exclamation points among rounded forms such as bee balm (*Monarda* species), garden phlox, cranesbills (*Geranium* species), and yarrow (*Achillea* species).

CULTIVARS AND RELATED SPECIES: Creamy wild indigo (*B. bracteata*, formerly *B. leucophaea*) produces compact 1- to 2-foot mounds of foliage with tightly packed, drooping clusters of creamy-yellow flowers. The 1- to 2-inch trilobed leaves are clothed in soft hairs. Look for this species in early spring before other species bloom. Plant in average, well-drained sandy or loamy soil in full sun or light shade. Found on sandy prairies, savannas, and in dry, open woods from Michigan and Minnesota, south to Kentucky and Texas. Zones 3 to 9.

Similar to blue false indigo, yellow wild indigo (*B. sphaerocarpa*, formerly *B. viridis*) has 6- to 8-inch flower spikes bearing bright lemon-yellow flowers. The plants are compact, with leafy stems to 3 feet. The fabulous round seedpods are dark gray-brown. Plant in average to rich, moist soil in full sun or light shade. Found in open woods and on roadsides in Arkansas and adjacent states. Zones 4 to 9.

Boltonia asteroides
WHITE BOLTONIA

Boltonia is a late-season perennial with tall mounds of asterlike flowers and lovely foliage. The wild form is seldom seen in cultivation—most gardeners know this plant only as the selection 'Snowbank'.

Plant boltonia in moist, humus-rich soil in full sun or light shade. In drier soil, plants will be smaller. Plants seldom need staking, but if you wish to keep plants short, cut them back to 10 or 12 inches in early June to encourage compact growth without sacrificing flowers. Overgrown plants should be divided in spring.

NATIVE HABITAT AND RANGE: Low, open woods, wetland margins, and wet ditches from New Jersey and North Dakota, south to Florida and Texas.

'Snowbank' is a neat, compact white boltonia smothered with bright flowers throughout the fall.

USDA HARDINESS ZONES: 3 to 8
HABIT, USE, AND COMPANIONS: The wealth of ghostly 1-inch white daisylike flowers with bright yellow centers are carried in mounded clusters on 4- to 6-foot stems clothed in gray-green, willowlike foliage that is attractive and neat all summer. Combine boltonias with summer- and fall-blooming plants such as fire weed (*Chamerion angustifolium*), joe-pye weeds (*Eutrochium* species), and iron-weeds (*Vernonia* species). In formal gardens, plant them with smooth

WILDFLOWERS FOR SUN

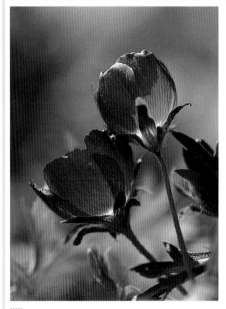

Winecups

aster, turtleheads, and Japanese anemones. Place them at the back of the border where the full mounds of foliage and flowers will not smother other plants.

CULTIVARS AND RELATED SPECIES: 'Pink Beauty' has a more open form and its pale pink flowers open several weeks before 'Snowbank'. Flower color is brighter where summers are cool. 'Snowbank' is a compact selection to 5 feet, smothered with bright white flowers throughout the fall.

Callirhoe involucrata
WINECUPS, POPPY MALLOW

Winecups are floriferous plants of the Southwest and Great Plains with five squared-off petals that together form a 2-foot flower resembling a teacup. The plants have weakly upright to trailing 1- to 3-foot stems clothed in attractive deeply dissected leaves. They begin blooming in spring and flower for several months on new growth.

Plant in average, well-drained loamy or sandy soil in full sun or light shade. Established plants have deep taproots that resent disturbance, so set out young plants and do not lift them once they are established.

NATIVE HABITAT AND RANGE: Dry, sandy plains, prairies, and open woods from North Dakota and Montana, south to Missouri and New Mexico; naturalized in the East.

USDA HARDINESS ZONES: 4 to 9

HABIT, USE, AND COMPANIONS: Sprawling stems make winecups an excellent weaver, best placed at the front of the border to knit together plantings. The trailing stems creep between or over clumps of plants, and flowers pop up here and there. In rich soils, plants form more dense clumps, good at the edge of a bed or along a path. In prairie gardens, plant them with prairie phlox (*Phlox pilosa*), blanket flower (*Gaillardia* species), and prickly pear (*Opuntia humifusa*). Let the trailing stems spill over a rock wall with sedums, hens and chicks (*Sempervivum* species), and lavender.

CULTIVARS AND RELATED SPECIES: Standing winecups (*C. digitata*) produce wiry, upright 1- to 4-foot stems and deeply dissected foliage with five to seven narrow, linear lobes resembling slender fingers. The burgundy-red flowers are borne singly or in open clusters. Some plants have white or light rose flowers. A mature clump in flower is a memorable sight. Plants thrive in well-drained loamy or sandy soil in full sun or light shade. They tend to flop in the shade but can be placed to grow up through large perennials or shrubs to support the sprawling stems. Found on dry prairies and in open woods from Missouri and Kansas, south to Texas; naturalized farther east. Zones 4 to 9.

Pale purple coneflower

Echinacea pallida
PALE PURPLE CONEFLOWER

Coneflowers are erect perennials with coarse, lance-shaped to oval leaves. The flamboyant, daisylike flowers have mounded, bristly heads and showy rose or pink petal-like rays held above the foliage. Coneflowers are used medicinally for alleviating skin rashes and stimulating the immune system.

Plant in average to rich, loamy or sandy soil in full sun or light shade. They grow best with adequate moisture but are quite tolerant of extended drought. Mature plants form stout clumps from deep, fleshy taproots that resent disturbance.

NATIVE HABITAT AND RANGE: Found in open woods, savannas, and prairies from Illinois to Iowa, south to Arkansas and Oklahoma. USDA HARDINESS ZONES: 4 to 8 HABIT, USE, AND COMPANIONS: Pale purple coneflower is a sparsely branching plant with stout, nearly leafless 2- to 4-foot stems topped with large heads of 4-inch drooping, pale rose rays. The basal leaves are lance-shaped and clothed in stiff hairs. Plant coneflowers in formal

WILDFLOWERS FOR SUN

gardens with garden phlox (*Phlox paniculata*), blazing stars (*Liatris* species), and globe thistles (*Echinops* species). In meadows and prairies, plant them with mountain mint (*Pycnanthemum* species), butterfly weed, and purple prairie clover (*Dalea purpurea*). The dried seed heads ornament the winter landscape.

CULTIVARS AND RELATED SPECIES: Narrow-leafed coneflower (*E. angustifolia*) is the shortest of the genus, with 1- to 2-foot stems and spare, lance-shaped basal leaves with stiff hairs. The mostly leafless stems are topped by 2-inch heads with drooping, rose-pink rays. Plants tolerate alkaline and saline soils. Found on dry prairies and savannas from Saskatchewan and Minnesota, south to Texas. Zones 2 to 8.

Yellow coneflower (*E. paradoxa*) is called paradoxical because its rays are bright yellow. The plants grow 2 to 3 feet tall in tight, multistemmed clumps with mostly basal, lance-shaped leaves. Found in open woods and prairies in the Ozark Mountains of Missouri and Arkansas. Zones 4 to 8.

Eutrochium purpureum
SWEET JOE-PYE WEED
Joe-pye weeds are big, bold peren-

nials with opposite or whorled leaves and clouds of small fuzzy flowers in terminal clusters. The plants form strong multistemmed clumps from stout crowns with tough, fibrous roots. The foliage is vanilla-scented when bruised.

Plant joe-pye weed in moist, average to rich soil in full sun or light shade. Established plants need little attention. Young plants reach their full, gargantuan size in two years.

NATIVE HABITAT AND RANGE: Seepage slopes, low meadows, woodland edges, and roadsides from New Hampshire to Iowa, south in the mountains to Georgia, and to Oklahoma.

USDA HARDINESS ZONES: 3 to 8
HABIT, USE, AND COMPANIONS: Sweet joe-pye weed forms beautiful clumps up to 6 feet tall with billowing crowns of pale rose or light purple flowers. The 12-inch leaves are carried in tiered whorls of four. Joe-pye weeds are equally suited to formal and informal landscapes with bee balms, coneflowers, lilies, sneezeweed, asters (*Symphyotrichum* species), goldenrods (*Solidago* species), and grasses. The skeletonized seed heads are attractive in the winter landscape.

CULTIVARS AND RELATED SPECIES: The 'Atropurpureum' variety is more compact than the wild form, with deep purple stems, dark leaves, and raspberry-red, sweetly scented flowers; it may be a hybrid with spotted joe-pye weed (*E. maculatum*). 'Big Umbrella' is a German selection with dark stems and huge heads of dark raspberry-red flowers. 'Gateway' is a 6-foot giant with mauve flower clusters the size of basketballs.

Spotted joe-pye weed is a relatively short species, from 4 to 6 feet, with compact, flattened clusters of pale cherry-red to rose-purple flowers. Found in wet prairies, bottomlands, and marshes from Newfoundland and British Columbia, south to Pennsylvania and Oklahoma; also in the moun-

tains to Georgia and New Mexico. Zones 2 to 8.

Gaura lindheimeri
WHITE GAURA

Gaura is an airy plant noted for its long blooming season and heat tolerance. Each flower consists of four petals that surround the protruding stamens, which resemble the antennae of a pure white butterfly.

Give gaura average to rich, moist, well-drained soil in full sun. Once established, plants are drought tolerant. Southern gardeners prize gaura because it tolerates heat and humidity with aplomb.

NATIVE HABITAT AND RANGE: Open, low woods, prairies,

White gaura tolerates heat well and blooms all summer and into the fall.

WILDFLOWERS FOR SUN

pinelands, and roadsides in Louisiana and Texas.

USDA HARDINESS ZONES: 5 to 9

HABIT, USE, AND COMPANIONS: White gaura is an exuberant, shrubby perennial with upright to lax, 3- to 4-foot stems carrying spikes of 1-inch white flowers in a cloud above the 3-inch deep green foliage. As the flowers age, they blush to pale rose. Gaura blooms all summer and into the autumn in clumps growing from a thick, deep taproot. Gaura is an excellent see-through plant for borders, meadow gardens, or as a specimen. Combine the airy whirl of flowers with ornamental grasses, blazing stars, butterfly weed, sunflowers, and coneflowers.

CULTIVARS AND RELATED SPECIES: Scarlet gaura (*G. coccinea*) is a daintier plant with 2-foot stems densely clothed in narrow, 1-inch leaves. Small rose-pink to red flowers crowd the tips of the stems in spring and early summer. Plant scarlet gaura in average to rich, well-drained soil in full sun. Found on dry prairie ridges, savannas, plains, and roadsides from Indiana and Alberta, south to Missouri, Texas, and California. Zones 3 to 9.

Helianthus angustifolius
SWAMP SUNFLOWER

Sunflowers are robust summer or autumn bloomers with stout, leafy stems from thick, tough rootstock. The brilliant yellow, daisylike flowers are arrayed in elongated clusters. Individual flowers have prominent, round centers. Birds love the seeds in the ripe heads.

Plant in moist, average to rich soil in full sun. It thrives in wet soil and tolerates drought once established. This large plant requires ample room to keep from crowding its neighbors and tends to flop in the wind or when grown in rich soil.

NATIVE HABITAT AND RANGE: Low woods, streambanks, bottomlands, and ditches from New York and Indiana, south to Florida and Texas, mostly along the coastal plain and the lower Mississippi River drainage.

USDA HARDINESS ZONES: 6 to 9; hardy farther north but does not bloom before frost

HABIT, USE, AND COMPANIONS: Swamp sunflower is a masterful plant with stout 4- to 10-foot stems crowned in September and October with elongated, branching clusters of 3-inch bright yellow flowers with purple centers. The deep green, lance-shaped leaves are showy in summer. Swamp sunflowers are indispensable additions to the fall garden. Plant them in a meadow or at the back of a large perennial garden. They make a great end-of-season show with the last of the goldenrods, asters, and grasses. CULTIVARS AND RELATED SPECIES: Willow leaf sunflower (*H. salicifolius*) is a delicate sunflower prized for its long, narrow, drooping, gray-green leaves as well as for its 2-inch flowers carried in slender, upright clusters throughout the autumn. Plant in average, sandy or loamy, neutral to alkaline, well-drained soil in full sun. Found on dry prairies, savannas, and roadsides from Illinois and Missouri to Kansas and Oklahoma. Zones 4 to 8.

Marsh mallow

Hibiscus moscheutos
MARSH MALLOW, ROSE MALLOW

Hibiscus are perennials of shrublike shape and proportions. The thick, erect stems are topped by open clusters of huge flowers, each with five petals that seem made of crepe paper with a long, central bottlebrush that bears the male and female reproductive structures. Their deeply cut, lacy leaves resemble those of maple. Individual flowers last only one day, but open in succession for three to six weeks. The woody seed capsules are quite attractive in fall and winter.

Plant in evenly moist, humus-rich soil in full sun or light shade. Space young transplants at least a yard apart to allow for their size when mature. Established plants are difficult to transplant and seldom need division. Japanese beetles may skeletonize the leaves; pick them off and drop them in a pail of soapy water. NATIVE HABITAT AND RANGE: Wet meadows, low woods, marshes, and ditches from Maryland and Ohio, south to Indiana and Texas. USDA HARDINESS ZONES: 5 to 10, 4 with protection

WILDFLOWERS FOR SUN

HABIT, USE, AND COMPANIONS:
Marsh mallow is a popular perennial
with broadly oval leaves with three
to five shallow lobes. The 6- to 8-inch
white flowers with deep red centers
are crowded at the upper ends of the
stems and open for several months
in summer. Plant mallows wherever
you need a bold dash of color. They
make great specimen plants for a
strong accent among shrubs, perennials, and ornamental grasses.
Around the margins of a pond, in a
pot in a water garden, or in a meadow, plant hibiscus with ferns, iris,
astilbes, and ironweed.

CULTIVARS AND RELATED SPECIES:
Marsh mallow (*H. moscheutos*
subsp. *palustris*) has three-lobed
leaves and rose-pink or white flowers without an eye. Its native range
is confined to coastal areas. Many
hybrids have been made combining
the compact growth of this species
and its color variants with the red
flowers of scarlet rose mallow (*H.
coccineus*). The hybrids have huge,
8- to 10-inch flowers in pure white,
white with a crimson eye, pink,
rose, and bright red. 'Sweet Caro-
line' has ruffled pink flowers with a
dark eye. 'Anne Arundel' has 9-inch
pink flowers. 'Lady Baltimore' is
pink with a deep red center. 'Lord
Baltimore' is deep scarlet.

Scarlet rose mallow (*H. coccineus*)
is a stately plant from 5 to 10 feet tall
with broad, deeply incised, palmately
lobed or divided leaves, often with
red-tinged margins. The 6-inch
saucer-shaped flowers are bright
scarlet. Found in wet woods,
swamps, and marshes on the coast of
Georgia and Florida. Zones 7 to 10.

Seaside mallow (*Kosteletzkya
virginica*) is a dainty hibiscus relative with 1- to 4-foot stalks bearing
soft, triangular leaves with a long,
pointed, central lobe. The flowers
resemble hibiscus, with 3-inch dark
pink flowers carried in clusters at
the tops of the stems. Plant in rich,
moist to wet soil in full sun. Found
in coastal marshes and ditches
from New York to Florida and west
to Texas. Zones 6 to 9.

Liatris pycnostachya
KANSAS GAYFEATHER, PRAIRIE BLAZING STAR

Liatris is a commanding plant with
tall stems bearing dozens of small
red-violet to purple flowers gath-
ered in dense spikes or buttonlike
clusters. The spikes open from the
top down, an unusual characteristic
for a perennial. The grasslike basal
leaves are longer and broader than
the stem leaves. As the leaves
ascend the stem, they reduce in
size until they blend into the flowers. Liatris is a popular cut flower.

Kansas gayfeather makes a striking statement blooming in midsummer.

Plant in rich, evenly moist soil in full sun. Plants are easily overgrown by large, floppy plants, so give them space without competition. The tall stalks may need staking. Mice and voles love to devour the corms.

NATIVE HABITAT AND RANGE: Prairies from Indiana and South Dakota, south to Louisiana and Texas.

USDA HARDINESS ZONES: 3 to 9

HABIT, USE, AND COMPANIONS: Kansas gayfeather is one of the largest and showiest species. The 3- to 5-foot spikes of densely packed, red-violet to mauve flower heads are carried on stiff, leafy stems. The deep green basal leaves are up to 12 inches long. It blooms in midsummer and is extremely showy when grown in clumps. In meadow and prairie gardens, plant it in the company of other natives such as golden Alexanders (*Zizia* species), prairie phlox, mountain mints, coneflowers, goldenrods, milkweeds (*Asclepias* species), and ornamental grasses. It adds striking vertical form to beds and borders, in contrast to summer-blooming perennials like yarrow and phlox.

CULTIVARS AND RELATED SPECIES: *Liatris pycnostachya* f. *alba*, also listed as 'Alba', has creamy-white flowers but is seed-grown and variable.

Button liatris (*L. ligulistylis*) has rounded heads of fuzzy, violet flow-

WILDFLOWERS FOR SUN

ers with purple bracts borne in open spikes and grows 2 to 5 feet tall. Plant in humus-rich, evenly moist soil in full sun. Found on wet black-soil prairies and the borders of marshes from Wisconsin and Alberta, south to Colorado and New Mexico. Zones 3 to 8.

Dotted blazing star (*L. punctata*) is a compact, densely clumping plant to 14 inches tall with small heads packed tightly into dense, 6-inch spikes in late summer. The attractive foliage is deep black-green. Plant in well-drained soil in full sun. Found on dry gravel prairies and plains from Manitoba and Alberta, south to Texas and New Mexico. Zones 2 to 8.

Monarda didyma
BEE BALM, OSWEGO TEA

Monardas boast brightly colored, spherical heads of tightly packed, tubular flowers above a circle of colored, leafy bracts. The 1-inch flowers have distinctive, protruding upper lips that arch over the smaller, lower ones. Like all mints, the stems of bee balm are square, the pointed, oval leaves are aromatic, and it growss from fast-creeping runners with fibrous roots. Many garden selections have been named, some of which are hybrids with bergamot (*M. fistulosa*).

Plant in humus-rich, evenly moist soils in full sun or partial shade. If plants dry out, they are more susceptible to powdery mildew. All monardas spread rapidly from creeping stems, and the clumps eventually die out in the center. Divide clumps every two or three years to keep them vigorous.

NATIVE HABITAT AND RANGE: Moist open woods, shaded roadsides, and clearings from Maine and Michigan, south to New Jersey and Ohio; in the mountains to Georgia. **USDA HARDINESS ZONES**: 3 to 8 **HABIT, USE, AND COMPANIONS**: Bee balm has brilliant 4-inch flower heads surrounded by deep red bracts attractive to gardeners and hummingbirds alike. The stout 2- to 4-foot succulent stems form tight clumps. In a moist spot in dappled shade, plant them with queen-of-the-prairie (*Filipendula rubra*), wild sennas (*Senna* species), turtleheads, ferns, hardy cranesbills, garden phlox, yarrows, and shasta daisies (*Leucanthemum* × *superbum*). **CULTIVARS AND RELATED SPECIES**: 'Blue Stocking' has soft, violet-blue flowers with bright violet bracts. 'Claire Grace' has lavender flowers. 'Jacob Klime' is deep red. 'Marshall's Delight' has clear pink flowers. All these cultivars are mildew resistant. The selection

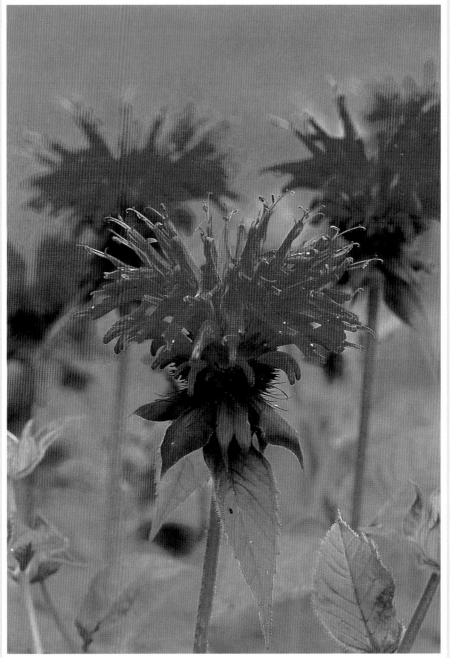

The brilliant red of bee balm attracts gardeners and hummingbirds alike.

WILDFLOWERS FOR SUN

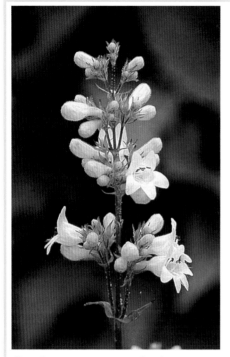

Foxglove penstemon, also known as beardtongue, is a tall wildflower that originates in wet meadows.

'Prairie Night' has red-violet flowers.

Lemon mint (*M. citriodora*) is a charming annual or biennial plant with soft, hairy, lemon-scented leaves on 2-foot stems. The 1½-inch, deep pink flowers are carried in whorled clusters where the leaves join the stems. They bloom throughout the summer. Plant in average sandy or loamy soil in full sun or light shade. Found in clearings, woodland edges, and plains from South Carolina and Missouri, south to Florida and Texas. Zones 4 to 9.

Penstemon digitalis
FOXGLOVE PENSTEMON

This wildflower, also known as beardtongue, is noted for its inflated, irregularly shaped flowers with two upper and three lower lips. The flowers vary from pink, rose, lavender, and violet to white. The seed capsules are decorative in fall and winter.

Plant in moist, rich soil in full sun or light shade. Plants quickly form dense clumps that need division every three or four years to keep them healthy. Self-sown seedlings will be numerous.

NATIVE HABITAT AND RANGE: Wet meadows and prairies, low woods, flood plains, and ditches from Nova Scotia and Minnesota, south to Virginia and Texas.
USDA HARDINESS ZONES: 3 to 8
HABIT, USE, AND COMPANIONS: Foxglove penstemon is a tall plant to 5 feet with open, branched clusters of 1-inch white flowers. The 6- to 8-inch, toothless shiny green leaves form tufted rosettes that grow from fibrous roots. In meadows and soggy spots, combine them with ferns, grasses, bee balm, oxeye (*Heliopsis helianthoides*), and ironweeds. In a formal garden, combine them with cranesbills, ornamental onions, yarrows, Siberian iris, and daylilies.

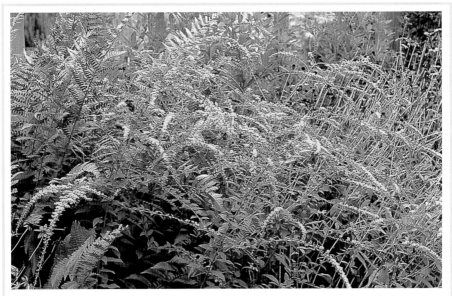

The arching branches of the spectacular rough-stemmed goldenrod create a chartreuse haze before the lemon-yellow flowers open in the autumn.

CULTIVARS AND RELATED SPECIES:
'Husker Red' has deep ruby-red foliage and stems and pink-tinged flowers.

Small's beardtongue (*P. smallii*) is a bushy penstemon with 2-foot stems clothed top to bottom in 1-inch, rose-purple flowers for several weeks in early spring. The glossy, broadly lance-shaped, 4-inch leaves have toothed margins. It must have good drainage, but is short-lived even under ideal conditions. Give it average, well-drained soil in full sun or light shade. Found in open woods, woodland margins, and cliffs in the southern Appalachians from North Carolina to Tennessee. Zones 6 to 8.

Solidago rugosa
ROUGH-STEMMED GOLDENROD

Goldenrods flower just as other blooms are slacking off in the garden. The lemon-yellow or golden flowers are carried in plumelike clusters on leafy stems. The silvery seed heads are lovely in early winter.

Plant in average to rich, moist soil in full sun or light shade. Plants spread enthusiastically from creeping rhizomes to form full, gorgeous clumps. Divide plants to control their spread.

NATIVE HABITAT AND RANGE:
Found in open woods, meadows, and old fields from Newfoundland

WILDFLOWERS FOR SUN

and Michigan, south to Florida and Texas.

USDA HARDINESS ZONES: 4 to 9.

HABIT, USE, AND COMPANIONS: Rough-stemmed goldenrod is a spectacular species with leafy arching branches from 1 to 3 1/2 feet tall and very broad, open flower clusters in October and November. The buds produce an attractive chartreuse haze before the flowers open. Choose rough-stemmed goldenrod for informal meadows and prairies or formal gardens with asters, sunflowers, phlox, anemones, and grasses. They are beautiful when contrasted with the tropical foliage of bananas, cannas, and elephant ears (*Colocasia* species).

CULTIVARS AND RELATED SPECIES: 'Fireworks' is a superior selection with long chains of flowers in full clusters.

Stiff goldenrod (*S. rigida*) is an unusual species that bears its flowers in large, flattened clusters, creating a showy display of yellow in the late-summer garden. Erect, multistemmed clumps rise 2 to 5 feet from a basal-foliage rosette. The softly hairy, oval foliage is attractive all season and turns dusty rose in autumn. Found on gravel or black-soil prairies, meadows, clearings, and roadsides from Connecticut to Saskatchewan, south to Georgia and New Mexico. Zones 3 to 9.

Solidago spathulata is a creeping goldenrod with deep green, paddle-shaped leaves and 1- to 2-foot inflorescences with stiff, horizontal branches. Plant in average to rich, moist soil in full sun or light shade. 'Golden Fleece' is only 12 inches tall and is quite floriferous. Found in open, rocky woods, clearings, and on roadsides in limy soils from Virginia and Indiana south to Georgia and Alabama. Zones 4 to 9.

Stokesia laevis
STOKES' ASTER

Blue is a valuable color and always at a premium in the garden. The showy 3- to 4-inch flat flower heads of Stokes' aster have two concentric rows of ragged blue rays and fuzzy white centers. The attractive buds resemble straw flowers.

Plant in average to rich, moist soil in full sun or light shade. Stokes' asters are easy-to-grow, long-lived perennials that form dense, multicrowned clumps. Divide for propagation or when plants get overcrowded.

NATIVE HABITAT AND RANGE: Low, wet pine woods, bottomlands, and ditches from North Carolina to Florida and Louisiana.

USDA HARDINESS ZONES: 5 to 9

HABIT, USE, AND COMPANIONS:
Stokes' aster has a broad rosette of shiny green, lance-shaped leaves, each of which has a conspicuous white midvein. Each 1- to 2-foot branched stalk bears several flowers in summer. Plants grow from cord-like white roots. Stokes' asters create a dramatic show for several months in summer. Combine them with small flowers and fine-textured foliage such as verbenas, penste-mons, yarrows, and ornamental grasses. In light shade plant them with phlox, columbines (*Aquilegia* species), ferns, and hostas.

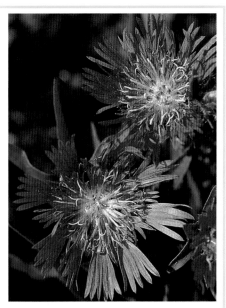
Stokes' aster

CULTIVARS AND RELATED SPECIES:
'Blue Danube' has 5-inch lavender-blue flowers, 'Blue Star' has deep sky-blue flowers. 'Silver Moon' has creamy-white flowers. 'Wyoming' has rich blue-violet flowers.

Symphyotrichum (formerly *Aster*) *novae-angliae*
NEW ENGLAND ASTER

The aster family contains some of the most beautiful and best-known roadside wildflowers and garden perennials. The flowers are so famil-iar and characteristic that similar flowers in many of its genera are referred to as "asterlike." New Eng-land aster is prized for its mounds of royal-purple flowers in late summer.

Plant New England aster in evenly moist, humus-rich soil in full sun or light shade. It will tolerate wet soil, but if it gets dry in sum-mer, the lower leaves will drop. It's also prone to flopping without the support of other large perennials and shrubs. To keep plants com-pact, shear them back to 8 or 12 inches in June. Bushy stems will resprout in time to set plenty of buds. Divide clumps every three to four years in spring or after flower-ing. New England asters are susceptible to powdery mildew, which turns the leaves dull gray. Keep plants from wilting, which gives the disease a foothold. Dust affected plants with sulfur to con-trol the spread of the disease.

WILDFLOWERS FOR SUN

New England aster 'Purple Dome' is a dwarf cultivar of the classic wildflower that blooms in gardens and along roadsides in late summer.

NATIVE HABITAT AND RANGE: Wet meadows, prairies, and pond margins from New England to North Dakota, south to Alabama and New Mexico.

USDA HARDINESS ZONES: 3 to 8

HABIT, USE, AND COMPANIONS: A meadow washed with purple New England asters in September is a memorable sight. Mature plants form dense 3- to 6-foot clumps with stiff, leafy stems crowned by dense clusters of 1- to 2-inch lavender to purple flowers with bright yellow centers. Flower color also varies from pure white to pink and rose. In the garden, combine New England asters with other fall-blooming wildflowers, such as goldenrod, sneezeweed (*Helenium autumnale*), gentians, and turtleheads (*Chelone* species). In borders, the height of most selections relegates them to the rear. Mix with Japanese anemones (*Anemone* × *hybrida*), beautyberry (*Callicarpa* species), and ornamental grasses.

CULTIVARS AND RELATED SPECIES: 'Alma Potschke' has rich, glowing salmon-pink flowers on compact 2- to 4-foot plants. Plants bloom in mid-fall. Another favorite is 'Barr's Pink', with semidouble bright rose-pink flowers in dense heads on

4-foot plants. 'Hella Lacy' has royal-purple flowers on tight, 3- to 4-foot clumps. 'Purple Dome' is a dwarf selection with royal-purple flowers on 2-foot, late-flowering clumps. 'September Ruby' has luscious red flowers on floppy 3- to 5-foot plants. 'Treasure' has a more open form and lavender-blue flowers on 4-foot stems.

Native smooth aster (*S. laeve*) is found in meadows, prairies, woodland edges, and roadsides from Maine to British Columbia, south to Georgia and New Mexico. It is a free-flowering species with lavender-blue flowers in open, elongated clusters on 2- to 3-foot plants, elegant in formal borders and in drifts in prairie and meadow gardens. This is one of the last flowers to bloom in autumn. 'Blue Bird' is a compact plant with deep sky-blue flowers. Zones 2 to 7.

Aromatic aster (*S. oblongifolium*), produces wide, low mounds of 1¼-inch purple flowers in September and October. The fuzzy, oblong foliage and scaly buds create an interesting display through the summer season. 'Dream of Beauty' is shorter in stature and has rose-pink flowers. 'Raydon's Favorite' is a southern cultivar with mounds of blue-purple flowers in October. Found on dry, sandy to rocky slopes in meadows, prairies, open woods, and roadsides from Pennsylvania to Saskatchewan, south to Alabama and New Mexico. Zones 3 to 8.

Thermopsis villosa (formerly T. caroliniana)
CAROLINA BUSH PEA

A Carolina bush pea in full bloom is an exceptional sight. Its narrow, upright stems and alternate gray-green leaves, fuzzy underneath, are crowned by tightly packed spikes of bright lemon-yellow flowers. Each leaf has three oval leaflets joined to a short stalk. The seed heads are showy in winter, and chickadees and sparrows relish the seeds.

Plant in average to rich, moist but well-drained acidic soil in full sun or light shade. In limy soils plants become anemic and yellow.
NATIVE HABITAT AND RANGE: Open woods, meadows, clearings, and roadsides from North Carolina to Georgia.
USDA HARDINESS ZONES: 3 to 9
HABIT, USE, AND COMPANIONS: Carolina bush peas have 3- to 5-foot stalks and showy yellow, pealike flowers. Plants form multistemmed clumps from woody, fibrous-rooted crowns. Place them in the middle or rear of borders with meadow rues (*Thalictrum* species), catmints

WILDFLOWERS FOR SUN

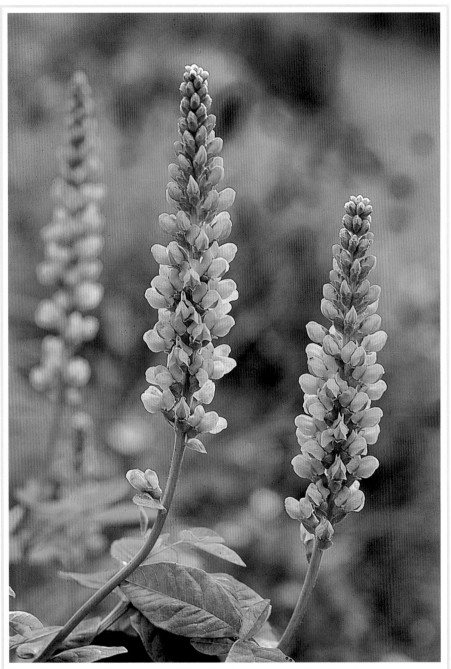

The tall, lemon-yellow spires of Carolina bush pea are dazzling in summer.

(*Nepeta* species), hardy cranesbills, phlox, and peonies. At the edge of a meadow or woodland, plant them with wild sennas, bluestar, bowman's-root, bergamot, and grasses.

CULTIVARS AND RELATED SPECIES: Growing 2 to 3 feet tall with vivid yellow flowers, mountain false lupine (*T. rhombifolia*) is found in wet meadows from Washington to Montana, south to Colorado and Nevada. Zones 4 to 8.

Tradescantia subaspera
SPIDERWORT

Spiderworts are named for the weblike hairs in the centers of the flowers. They produce hundreds of attractive satiny, three-petaled flowers in clusters atop succulent, jointed stems. Flower colors vary from purple, lavender, and blue to pink, rose-red, and white. Each flower lasts only half a day, closing by early afternoon.

Plant in average to rich, moist but well-drained soil in full to light shade. Plants grow well in partial shade but do not flower as long. After flowering the clumps flop, so cut them to the ground. They produce new foliage in late summer or autumn. Plants increase quickly to form dense clumps and self-sow readily.

NATIVE HABITAT AND RANGE: Rich woods, clearings, and roadsides from Virginia and Illinois, south to Florida and Alabama.

USDA HARDINESS ZONES: 4 to 9

HABIT, USE, AND COMPANIONS: Spiderwort (*T. subaspera*) is the largest and stoutest of the spiderworts. Plants grow to $3^1/_2$ feet from thick, upright stems with broad, gray-green leaves and 1-inch blue to purple flowers. Plant spiderworts in formal gardens with hardy cranesbills, bergenias, phlox, and ornamental grasses. In meadows or woodland edges, plant them in drifts or scattered clumps with persistent plants like wild bleeding heart, mountain mints, bluestars, goldenrods, and ferns.

CULTIVARS AND RELATED SPECIES: Virginia spiderwort (*T. virginiana*) is a delicate plant with slender 2- to 3-foot stems and 12-inch deep green leaves. The flowers are blue to purple. Found in moist, open woods, flood plains, meadows, and prairies from Maine and Wisconsin, south to Georgia and Missouri. Zones 4 to 9.

Vernonia gigantea
TALL IRONWEED

The broad, violet flower clusters of ironweed demand attention in the summer and autumn garden. Most species have numerous tall, stiff stems clothed in deep green, lance-shaped leaves. The name ironweed

WILDFLOWERS FOR SUN

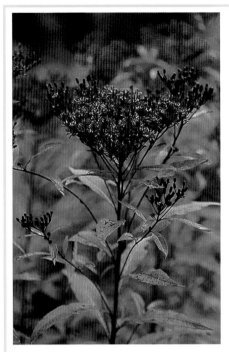

Tall ironweed

USDA HARDINESS ZONES: 4 to 8

HABIT, USE, AND COMPANIONS: Tall ironweed is the giant of the group, with 4- to 10-foot stems and dense, broad, flattened clusters of soft-violet flowers in late summer and autumn. Plant in rich, moist soil in full sun. Ironweeds are commanding border plants. Plant them with yarrows (*Achillea* species), cannas, lilies, salvias, and iris. They are equally well suited to meadow and prairie gardens or along the banks of ponds. Combine them with hibiscus, phlox, blue lobelia (*Lobelia siphilitica*), joe-pye weeds, turtleheads, asters, goldenrods, and grasses.

CULTIVARS AND RELATED SPECIES: *Vernonia angustifolia,* narrow-leaf ironweed, has small, deep violet flower heads carried in broad, open clusters on wide, shrublike clumps from 2 to 4 feet tall. The 6- to 8-inch leaves are narrowly lance-shaped and droop slightly on the stem. Found in sandy meadows, open woods, savannas, and roadsides from North Carolina to Florida and Mississippi. Zones 4 to 9.

presumably arises from the prominent rust-red hairs in the spent flower heads and on the fruits. Plants are grown from woody, fibrous-rooted crowns.

Plant in rich, evenly moist soil in full sun or light shade. Ironweed is easy to grow and thrives in most garden situations. The clumps get tall and wide but seldom need staking or division.

NATIVE HABITAT AND RANGE: Found in wet meadows and prairies, wetland edges, pond margins, and ditches from New York, Michigan, and Nebraska, south to Georgia and Louisiana.

Veronicastrum virginicum
CULVER'S ROOT
This plant's erect, creamy white candelabra spikes on stout 3- to 6-foot stems make a dramatic show.

The toothed, lance-shaped leaves are borne in tiered whorls on the stems. Culver's root is often placed in the genus *Veronica*, to which it is closely related.

Plant in rich, moist soil in full sun or light shade. Established plants tolerate short periods of drought. Plants form dense, multi-stemmed clumps that are easily divided in early spring or autumn. The dried seed heads ornament the winter landscape.

NATIVE HABITAT AND RANGE: Open woods, low meadows, prairies, floodplains, and outcroppings from Ontario and Manitoba, south to Georgia and Louisiana.

USDA HARDINESS ZONES: 3 to 9

HABIT, USE, AND COMPANIONS: The upright spikes of culver's root add lift and excitement to the middle or rear of beds and borders. Plants grow from woody crowns with thick, fleshy roots. In borders and formal situations combine them with turtleheads, hibiscus, coneflowers, and yarrows. Try milkweeds, bee balms, ironweeds, anise hyssop (*Agastache foeniculum*), rattlesnake master (*Eryngium yuccifolium*), asters, goldenrods, and grasses in meadow and prairie gardens.

CULTIVARS AND RELATED SPECIES: *Veronicastrum virginicum* 'Rosea',

Culver's root

sometimes listed as 'Roseum', has pale rose-pink flowers. Soft blue selections are seen but are likely to be from the European species.

Yucca filamentosa
THREAD-LEAF YUCCA, ADAM'S NEEDLE

Yuccas are quintessential desert plants, but they grow throughout North America. They produce clusters of bell-like white flowers on tall stems and rosettes of sword-shaped, blue-green leaves.

Plant yuccas in average to rich, well-drained soil in full sun or light shade. They are long-lived, drought tolerant, and carefree. After flowering, the main crown dies, but the

WILDFLOWERS FOR SUN

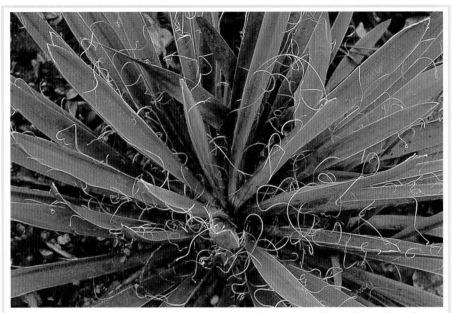

Thread-leaf yucca is a quintessential desert plant—long-lived, drought tolerant, and carefree.

rhizome produces auxiliary shoots that perpetuate the clump.

NATIVE HABITAT AND RANGE: Sand dunes, outcroppings, and pine barrens in mountains and the coastal plain from Maryland to Georgia.

USDA HARDINESS ZONES: 4 to 10

HABIT, USE, AND COMPANIONS: The erect, multibranched bloom stalks rise 5 to 15 feet above the stiff, 2- to $2^1/_2$-foot needlelike leaves. The nodding, creamy-white flowers are waxy in texture and are 2 inches long. Yucca grows from a woody crown with fleshy roots. Plant it in dry soil or rock gardens, as accent plantings, or in seaside gardens. Contrast the stiff foliage with soft or delicate plants such as verbenas, winecups, prickly pear cactus (*Opuntia humifusa*), sages, gaura, gaillardia, and evening primrose (*Oenothera* species).

CULTIVARS AND RELATED SPECIES: 'Bright Edge' has yellow-variegated leaves. Soapweed (*Y. glauca*) has narrow, 2-foot, stiff, gray-green leaves crowned by dense clusters of nodding, creamy-white to pale pink flowers on 2- to 3-foot stems. Plant in average to rich, well-drained soil in full sun or light shade. Found on dry prairies and plains from North Dakota and Wyoming, south to Missouri, Texas, and Arizona. Zones 3 to 9.

The American Woodland Garden
Rick Darke
Timber Press, 2002

**Bird Gardens: Welcoming
Wild Birds to Your Yard**
Stephen W. Kress, editor
Brooklyn Botanic Garden, 1998

Creating a Wildflower Meadow
Henry W. Art
Storey Press, 1988

The Environmental Gardener
Janet Marinelli, editor
Brooklyn Botanic Garden, 1992

Ferns for American Gardens
John Mickel
MacMillan, 1994

**Ferns: Wild Things Make a
Comeback in the Garden**
C. Colston Burrell, editor
Brooklyn Botanic Garden, 1994, 1995

**A Garden of Wildflowers:
101 Native Species and
How to Grow Them**
Henry W. Art
Storey Communications, 1986.

**A Gardener's Encyclopedia of
Wildflowers: An Organic Guide to
Choosing and Growing Over 150
Beautiful Wildflowers**
C. Colston Burrell
Rodale Press, 1997

Gardening with Native Wild Flowers
Samuel Jones and Leonard Foote
Timber Press, 1997

**Gardening with Native Plants of
the South**
Sally Wasowski with Andy Wasowski
Taylor Publishing Company, 1994

Gardening With Prairie Plants
Sally Wasowski With Andy Wasowski
University of Minnesota Press, 2002

**Going Native: Biodiversity in Our
Own Backyards**
Janet Marinelli, editor
Brooklyn Botanic Garden, 1994, 1996

**Herbaceous Perennial Plants:
A Treatise on Their Identification,
Culture, and Garden Attributes**
Allan Armitage
Varsity Press, 1989

**How to Grow Wildflowers and
Wild Shrubs and Trees in Your
Own Garden**
Hal Bruce
Knopf, 1976

**Jewels of the Plains:
Wildflowers of the Great Plains
Grasslands and Hills**
Claude A. Barr
University of Minnesota Press, 1983

**Native Perennials:
North American Beauties**
Nancy Beaubaire, editor
Brooklyn Botanic Garden, 1996

The Natural Habitat Garden
Druse, Kenneth with Margaret Roach
Clarkson Potter, 1994

Natural Landscaping: Designing With Native Plant Communities
John Diekelmann and Robert Schuster
McGraw-Hill, 1982

The Natural Lawn & Alternatives
Margaret Roach, editor
Brooklyn Botanic Garden, 1993

The Natural Water Garden: Pools Ponds, Marshes & Bogs for Backyards Everywhere
C. Colston Burrell, editor
Brooklyn Botanic Garden, 1997

Naturalistic Gardening: Reflecting the Planting Patterns of Nature
Ann Lovejoy
Sasquatch Books, 1998

New England Wild Flower Society Guide to Growing and Propagating Wildflowers of the United States and Canada
William Cullina
Houghton Mifflin, 2000

Perennials (2 volumes)
Roger Phillips and Martyn Rix
Random House, 1991

Pioneering With Wildflowers
George D. Aiken
Prentice-Hall, 1968, 1996

The Prairie Garden: 70 Native Plants You Can Grow in Town or Country
J. Robert Smith with Beatrice S. Smith
University of Wisconsin Press, 1980

Siftings
Jens Jensen
Johns Hopkins University Press, 1939, 1990

The Wildflower Gardener's Guide: Northeast, Mid-Atlantic, Great Lakes, and Eastern Canada
Henry W. Art
Storey/Garden Way Publishing, 1987

The Wildflower Gardener's Guide: Midwest, Great Plains, and Canadian Prairies
Henry W. Art
Storey/Garden Way Publishing, 1991

The Wildflower Meadow Book: A Gardener's Guide
Laura C. Martin
Globe Pequot Press, 1990

Wildflower Perennials for Your Garden: A Detailed Guide to Years of Bloom From America's Long-neglected Native Heritage
Bebe Miles
Hawthorne Books, 1976

Wildflowers in Your Garden
Vicki Ferreniea
Random House, 1993

The Woodland Garden
Roy Forster
Firefly Books, 2004

Woodland Gardens: Shade Gets Chic
C. Colston Burrell, editor
Brooklyn Botanic Garden, 1995

Forestfarm
990 Tetherow Road
Williams, OR 97544
541-846-7269
www.forestfarm.com

Landscape Alternatives, Inc.
25316 St. Croix Trail
Shafer, MN 55074
651-257-4460
www.landscapealternatives.com

Meadowbrook Nursery
We-Du Natives
2055 Polly Spout Road
Marion, NC 28752
828-738-8300; www.we-du.com

Missouri Wildflowers Nursery
9814 Pleasant Hill Road
Jefferson City, MO 65109
573-496-3492
www.mowildflowers.net

Native Gardens
5737 Fisher Lane
Greenback, TN 37742
865-856-0220
www.native-gardens.com

The Natural Garden
38 W. 443 Highway 64
St. Charles, IL 60175
630-584-0150
www.thenaturalgardeninc.com

Niche Gardens
1111 Dawson Road
Chapel Hill, NC 27516
919-967-0078
www.nichegardens.com

Plants of the Southwest
3095 Agua Fria Road
Santa Fe, NM 87507
800-788-7333
www.plantsofthesouthwest.com

Prairie Moon Nursery
Rt. 3, Box 163
Winona, MN 55987
507-452-1362
www.prairiemoon.com

Prairie Nursery
P.O. Box 306
Westfield, WI 53964
800-476-9453
www.prairienursery.com

Prairie Restorations, Inc.
P.O. Box 327
Princeton, MN 55371
763-389-4342
www.prairieresto.com

Sunlight Gardens
174 Golden Lane
Andersonville, TN 37705
800-272-7396
www.sunlightgardens.com

Transplant Nursery
County Road 315.
Green Cove Springs, FL 32043
904-284-0954
www.transplantnursery.com

Woodlanders, Inc.
1128 Colleton Avenue
Aiken, SC 29801
803-648-7522
www.woodlanders.net

HENRY W. ART is a garden writer, Samuel Fessenden Clarke Professor of Biology, and the director of the Center for Environmental Studies at Williams College in Williamstown, Massachusetts. He is the author of *Woods Walk: Peepers, Porcupines & Exploding Puffballs!* (with M.W. Robbins, 2003), two regional editions of *The Wildflower Gardener's Guide* (1987, 1991), *Creating a Wildflower Meadow* (1988), and *A Garden of Wildflowers: 101 Native Species and How to Grow Them* (1986). He has a doctorate in forestry from Yale University.

C. COLSTON BURRELL is a garden designer, photographer, naturalist, and award-winning author who has lived and gardened in the Midwest and the mid-Atlantic region. A self-described "chlorophyll addict," he currently gardens on ten acres in the Blue Ridge Mountains near Charlottesville, Virginia, and is principal of Native Landscape Design and Restoration, which specializes in blending nature and culture through artistic design. Burrell has published several best-selling books on gardening, including the award-winning *Gardener's Encyclopedia of Wildflowers* (1997). He also writes regularly for such publications as *Fine Gardening, Horticulture, Landscape Architecture,* and *American Gardener.* He has edited or contributed to 14 Brooklyn Botanic Garden handbooks, including *Native Alternatives to Invasive Plants* (2006), *Intimate Gardens* (2005), *The Sunny Border* (2002), *The Shady Border* (1998), *The Natural Water Garden* (1997), *Woodland Gardens* (1995), and *Ferns* (1994, 1995).

KIM HAWKS is a wildflower gardener who founded her own nursery, Niche Gardens, when she discovered that the only wildflowers available were either poor quality or had been dug from the wild. Niche Gardens in Chapel Hill, North Carolina, is a leading mail order nursery, growing North American natives with an emphasis on southeastern perennials. She is also a garden designer and writer, whose articles have appeared in *Fine Gardening, The Herb Companion, North Carolina Wildlife,* and *Carolina Gardener.*

JOAN FEELY is the curator of the Native Plant Collection, in charge of the naturalistic gardens of Fern Valley, at the U.S. National Arboretum. Before joining the Washington, D.C.–based arboretum in 1986, she lived and gardened in New York, Maine, Massachusetts, and Alaska.

MADELEINE KEEVE, who died in 2002, lived and gardened in Portland, Oregon. Before moving to Portland, she was a gardener at Wave Hill in the Bronx, New York. In addition to *Wildflower Gardens,* she also contributed to the BBG handbook *Gardener's World of Bulbs* (1991) and other publications, including *Low-Maintenance Gardening* (1998) and *Horticulture* magazine.

CAROLE OTTESEN is a garden writer and designer whose work has appeared in many magazines, including *House Beautiful, Horticulture, Garden Design*, and *Fine Gardening*. Her latest book is *The Herbal Epicure: Growing, Harvesting, and Cooking Healing Herbs* (2001). She is also the author of *The Native Plant Primer* (1995), *Ornamental Grasses: The Amber Wave* (1989, 1995), *Gardening With Style* (with Graham Rose and Peter King, 1988), and *The New American Garden* (1988). Her two-acre organic garden in Potomac, Maryland, includes ornamental grasses, several perennial borders, a medicinal plants garden, an herb and vegetable garden, a natural woodland garden, a moss lawn, and a vast array of plants, including many native to eastern North America.

JAMES STEVENSON has worked as assistant curator of hardy collections at the University of Oxford Botanic Garden and Harcourt Arboretum; at the Royal Botanic Gardens, Kew, in London; as curator and garden manager of Juniper Level Botanic Garden near Raleigh, North Carolina; at Fearington Gardens in Pittsboro, North Carolina; and at the North Carolina Botanical Garden in Chapel Hill. He earned a degree in plant ecology from the University of the South in Sewanee, Tennessee.

PHOTO CREDITS

C. COLSTON BURRELL: pages 8 (right), 20, 42, 43, 54, 58, 59, 87, 91, and 98

DAVID CAVAGNARO: pages 5, 10, 13, 21, 24, 27, 31, 33, 35, 37, 39, 45, 47, 61, 65, 62, 67, 68, 72, 80, 81, 83, 93, 96, and 99

ALAN & LINDA DETRICK: pages 29, 38 (left), 49, 50, 51, 60, 64, 75, 79, 89, and 94

CHRISTINE M. DOUGLAS: pages 9 (right) and 15

SUSAN M. GLASCOCK: pages 7, 9 (left), 48, 71, 77, 85, and 90

PAMELA HARPER: pages 44, 56, 63, and 100

CAROLE OTTESEN: pages 28 and 53

JERRY PAVIA: cover, pages 1, 8 (left), 14, 23, 34, 38 (right), 57, 66, 73, and 74

VIRGINIA R. WEILER: page 19

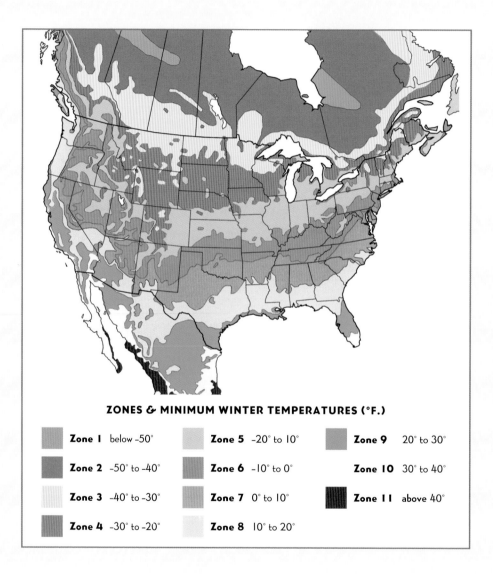

ZONES & MINIMUM WINTER TEMPERATURES (°F.)

Zone 1 below –50°

Zone 2 –50° to –40°

Zone 3 –40° to –30°

Zone 4 –30° to –20°

Zone 5 –20° to 10°

Zone 6 –10° to 0°

Zone 7 0° to 10°

Zone 8 10° to 20°

Zone 9 20° to 30°

Zone 10 30° to 40°

Zone 11 above 40°

INDEX

INDEX

PROVIDING EXPERT GARDENING ADVICE FOR OVER 60 YEARS

Join Brooklyn Botanic Garden as an annual Subscriber Member and receive our next three gardening handbooks delivered directly to you, plus *Plants & Gardens News*, *BBG Members News*, and reciprocal privileges at many botanic gardens across the country. Visit www.bbg.org/subscribe for details.

Brooklyn Botanic Garden All-Region Guides

World renowned for pioneering gardening information, Brooklyn Botanic Garden's award-winning guides provide practical advice in a compact format for gardeners in every region of North America. To order other fine titles, call 718-623-7286 or shop online at shop.bbg.org. For additional information about Brooklyn Botanic Garden, call 718-623-7200 or visit www.bbg.org.